TRAGEDY in SOUTH LEBANON:
THE ISRAELI-HEZBOLLAH WAR of 2006

CATHY SULTAN

Best wishes Helenta,

Cathy

SCARLETTA PRESS

MINNEAPOLIS

For information, visit our website at www.scarlettapress.com.

Library of Congress
Cataloging-in-Publication Data

Sultan, Cathy.

Tragedy in South Lebanon : the Israeli-Hezbollah war of 2006 / Cathy Sultan. -- 1st ed.

p.   cm.

Includes index.

ISBN 13: 978-0-9798249-1-3
ISBN 10: 0-9798249-1-5

(trade paper : alk. paper)
1. Lebanon War, 2006. I. Title.
DS87.65.S85 2007
956.9204'4--dc22
2007043708

For further information about *Tragedy in South Lebanon* and other Cathy Sultan endeavors, including contact information, go to the author's webpage at www.cathysultan.com.

The opinions contained within are that of the author and not necessarily Scarletta Press. Due to the rapidly shifting nature of events in the Middle East, situations and interpretations may change after March 2008.

ALSO BY CATHY SULTAN:
A Beirut Heart: One Woman's War
Israeli and Palestinian Voices

Book design by
Mighty Media Inc., Minneapolis, MN
Cover: Oona Gaarder-Juntti
Interior: Chris Long

10 9 8 7 6 5 4 3 2 1

Printed in Canada

"Tragedy in South Lebanon *provides vital information about a topic often misreported by the mainstream media. I particularly liked the interviews with both Hezbollah and Israeli soldiers describing the same battle. This is an important book that should be read by anyone interested in Israel and Lebanon.*"

"*As someone who works with other organizations to ban the use, sale, and transfer of cluster bombs, I applaud Cathy Sultan's discussion on the effects of these lethal weapons on Lebanese civilians, many of them children, who continue to be killed and maimed by these odious, unexploded Israeli cluster munitions.*"

"*Finally finally finally there is a book that looks at the complex issues in Lebanon for what they are – complex. And even more importantly, Sultan has taken her experience and transported all of us into the region to better understand the complexities from the people themselves. We have had enough of the bumper sticker slogans and five second sound bites. Great!*"

"*Sultan gives a fair and accurate account of what went on in South Lebanon. As a UN official who has spent 24 years in South Lebanon, I say she also lends refreshing voice to those who would otherwise never be heard.*"

Together we will work to support courage where there is fear,
foster agreement where there is conflict,
and inspire hope where there is despair.

NELSON MANDELA,
JULY 18, 2007

JOHANNESBURG, SOUTH AFRICA

CONTENTS

UNDOF: United Nations Disengagement Observation Force Zone

UNFIL: United Nations Force in Lebanon

North

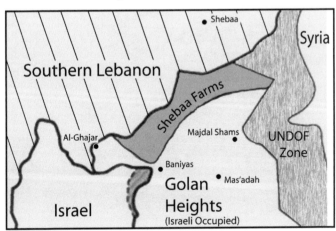

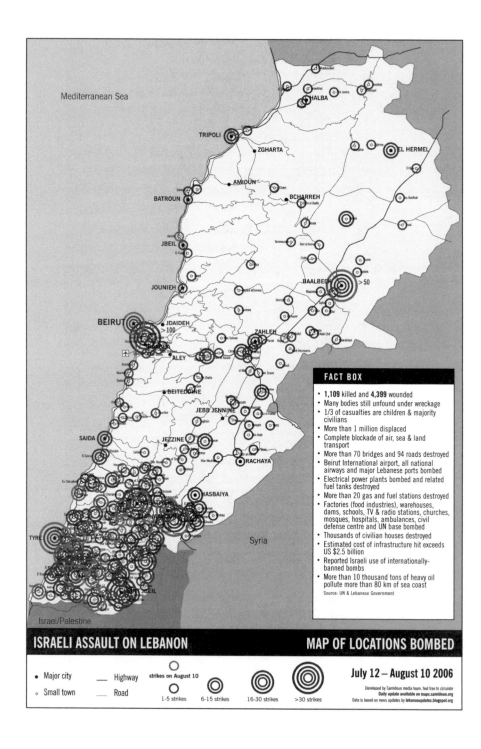

ISRAELI ASSAULT ON LEBANON

MAP OF LOCATIONS BOMBED

Mediterranean Sea

HALBA

TRIPOLI

ZGHARTA

EL HERMEL

AMIOUN

BCHARREH

BATROUN

JBEIL

JOUNIEH

BAALBECK >50

BEIRUT

JDAIDEH >100

ZAHLEH

ALEY

BEITEDDINE

JEBB JENNINE

SAIDA

JEZZINE

RACHAYA

HASBAIYA

TYRE

BEIL

Syria

Israel/Palestine

FACT BOX

- **1,109** killed and **4,399** wounded
- Many bodies still unfound under wreckage
- 1/3 of casualties are children & majority civilians
- More than 1 million displaced
- Complete blockade of air, sea & land transport
- More than 70 bridges and 94 roads destroyed
- Beirut International airport, all national airways and major Lebanese ports bombed
- Electrical power plants bombed and related fuel tanks destroyed
- More than 20 gas and fuel stations destroyed
- Factories (food industries), warehouses, dams, schools, TV & radio stations, churches, mosques, hospitals, ambulances, civil defense centre and UN base bombed
- Thousands of civilian houses destroyed
- Estimated cost of infrastructure hit exceeds US $2.5 billion
- Reported Israeli use of internationally-banned bombs
- More than 10 thousand tons of heavy oil pollute more than 80 km of sea coast

Source: UN & Lebanese Government

- Major city
- Small town
- Highway
- Road

strikes on August 10

1-5 strikes 6-15 strikes 16-30 strikes >30 strikes

July 12 – August 10 2006

Developed by Samidoun media team, feel free to circulate
Daily update available on maps.samidoun.org
Data is based on news updates by lebanonupdates.blogspot.com

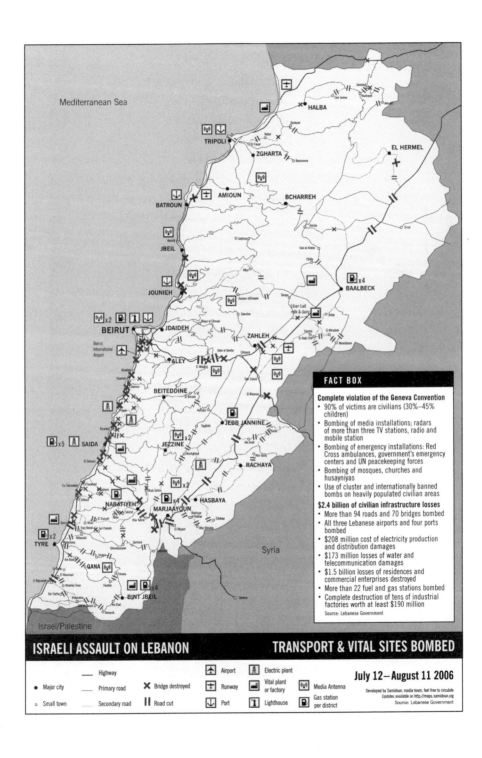

Mediterranean Sea

HALBA

TRIPOLI

ZGHARTA

EL HERMEL

BATROUN

AMIOUN

BCHARREH

JBEIL

BAALBECK x4

JOUNIEH

BEIRUT x2

JDAIDEH

ZAHLEH

Beirut International Airport

ALEY

BEITEDDINE

JEBB JANNINE

SAIDA x5

JEZZINE x2

RACHAYA

NABATIYEH x4

MARJAAYOUN

HASBAYA

TYRE x2

QANA x2

BINT JBEIL x4

Syria

Israel/Palestine

FACT BOX

Complete violation of the Geneva Convention
- 90% of victims are civilians (30%–45% children)
- Bombing of media installations; radars of more than three TV stations, radio and mobile station
- Bombing of emergency installations: Red Cross ambulances, government's emergency centers and UN peacekeeping forces
- Bombing of mosques, churches and husayniyas
- Use of cluster and internationally banned bombs on heavily populated civilian areas

$2.4 billion of civilian infrastructure losses
- More than 94 roads and 70 bridges bombed
- All three Lebanese airports and four ports bombed
- $208 million cost of electricity production and distribution damages
- $173 million losses of water and telecommunication damages
- $1.5 billion losses of residences and commercial enterprises destroyed
- More than 22 fuel and gas stations bombed
- Complete destruction of tens of industrial factories worth at least $190 million

Source: Lebanese Government

ISRAELI ASSAULT ON LEBANON

TRANSPORT & VITAL SITES BOMBED

Highway	Airport	Electric plant
Major city / Primary road	Runway	Vital plant or factory / Media Antenna
Small town / Secondary road / Road cut	Port	Lighthouse / Gas station per district
Bridge destroyed		

July 12 – August 11 2006

Developed by Samidoun, media team, feel free to circulate
Updates available on http://maps.samidoun.org
Source: Lebanese Government

Map 4140 Rev.1 United Nations
July 2006

x

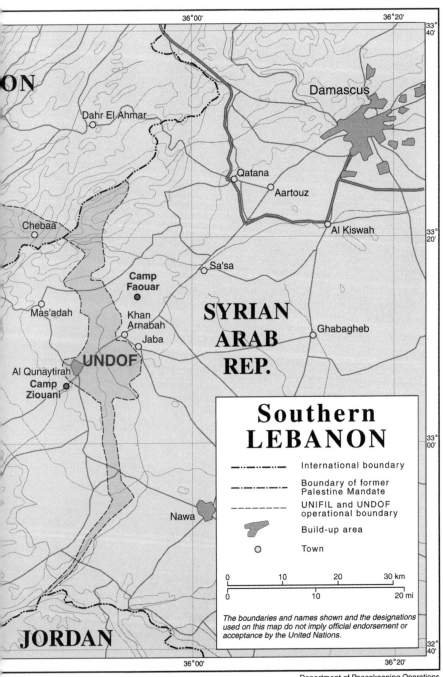

Southern LEBANON

—··—··—··	International boundary
—·—·—·—·	Boundary of former Palestine Mandate
— — — —	UNIFIL and UNDOF operational boundary
	Build-up area
○	Town

0 10 20 30 km

0   10   20 mi

The boundaries and names shown and the designations used on this map do not imply official endorsement or acceptance by the United Nations.

Damascus

Dahr El Ahmar

Qatana

Aartouz

Chebaa

Al Kiswah

Sa'sa

Camp Faouar

Mas'adah

Khan Arnabah

Jaba

SYRIAN ARAB REP.

Ghabagheb

UNDOF

Al Qunaytirah

Camp Ziouani

Nawa

JORDAN

APRIL 18, 1996

It is late afternoon in the tiny village of Qana, six kilometers south-east of Tyre in South Lebanon. The United Nation's blue and white flag hanging over the compound usually billows in the breeze. Today, its torn scraps snap harshly at the same light wind, signaling something is horribly amiss.

The prequel to this particular day starts five days earlier when the Israel Air Force begins an aerial bombing campaign across Lebanon called "Grapes of Wrath." It is meant to pressure the Lebanese government to disarm Hezbollah, which is resisting Israel's occupation of South Lebanon. Between April 13 and April 18, on orders from the Israeli military, some eight thousand civilians from the area around Qana flee their homes for points north. Eight hundred residents, who are either too poor or too old to flee, take shelter in a conference room in the center of the UN camp. Under the protection of this international body they assume they are safe.

At approximately 2:00 P.M., the Israeli military begins shelling the compound. With 155 mm. artillery fire, they hit from all sides, trapping the people so no one can flee. Then they target the conference center. The shelling lasts seventeen minutes. Those not killed outright burn to death when the conference center's roof caves in on top of them. In all, 106 Lebanese die.[1]

....

1   Seelye, Kate. "Face to Face with the Victims of State-Sponsored Israeli Terror at Qana." *Washington Report on Middle East Affairs*, July 1996, pp. 6–7.

The gravesite is at the base of the UN compound. The coffins, encased in mortar and cement and mounted atop slabs, are arranged horizontally in rows of six. Photos of the dead are placed atop each coffin. Along the camp's chain-link fence directly behind the gravesite, black mourning banners sway in the breeze. Family members and friends, there to pay their respects, pray silently beside the deceased. As a farewell gesture they leave behind bouquets of white lilies and jasmine. Their melancholic, sweet fragrance lingers in the air.

When I arrive at the gravesite, I am handed an album with some twenty-five photos taken shortly after the air strike. In one, a charred body smolders. In another, the upper torso of a young child lies on a table, headless.

"Who is that man?" I asked as I walked away. "Why did he give me those photos?"

"He's from Hezbollah," explains Elie, my escort. "I told him you were a writer. He asks you to please tell the story of the people of South Lebanon so they will not be forgotten."

. . .

For ten years I could find no context in which to write specifically about South Lebanon. Then, into the second week of the July 2006 conflict, Qana was hit again. This time the target was an apartment building. The thirty victims were from two families, the Shalhoubs and the Hashems. They had recently moved to the house on the edge of a high ridge. They thought it would be safer. Its position, at least, helped muffle the sounds of the bombs falling nearby. They discussed leaving several times but they were too poor and too numerous, fifty-six in all. The taxi fare north, around one thousand dollars, was unaffordable.[2] Israel contended that Hezbollah's ability to continue to attack Israel meant that its militia was being re-supplied. Qana is a crossroads, the junction of five sepa-

....

2   Tavernise, Sabrina. "There's Nobody Left in Our Village." *St. Paul Pioneer Press*, July 31, 2005.

rate highways and in the heart of Hezbollah territory, hence a legitimate target regardless of the innocent civilians living there.

I felt sick. Had I written about Qana before, would some angel have noticed and averted the bombs this second time and spared the lives of the innocent children and their parents? Of course not. There are no angels in South Lebanon.

For sixty years, the people of the south have been treated like outcasts and abandoned by their government. During the fourteen years I lived in Lebanon I was just as guilty as most Lebanese about my feelings toward the south. During Lebanon's civil war when some tragedy befell the area, I dare not admit how many times I said, "Who cares. The south isn't our problem." It was, of course. So now, in telling their story, I have a chance to pay homage to the people I slighted those many years ago.

The July 2006 war saw a rare moment of national unity for all Lebanese in the face of Israeli aggression against the people in South Lebanon. The rest of the country took notice of places like Bint Jbeil, Maroun al Ras, Aita al Sha'ab and Yaroun – villages most Lebanese knew nothing about, places where people struggled to survive when they were completely cut off from the rest of the country during twenty-two years of Israeli occupation, places that were carpet bombed into rubble in the 2006 war. In Aita al Sha'ab seven hundred fifty homes were completely destroyed, in Bint Jbeil the number exceeded eight hundred.[3]

. . .

The summer war of 2006 between Israel and Hezbollah produced a human catastrophe in Lebanon that killed 1,109 civilians and wounded an additional 4,399. To a smaller but no less tragic extent, Israelis in the Galilee feared for their lives as Hezbollah lobbed some four thousand rockets on their towns and villages, eight hundred of which landed in residential or com-

....

3   Human Rights Watch. http://hrw.org/reports/2007/lebanon0907/3.htm

mercial areas. These attacks killed thirty-nine civilians, eighteen of whom were Israeli Arabs. An additional four Israelis died of heart attacks. Of the 4,262 Israelis wounded, thirty-three of those were serious enough to require hospitalization. Some 2,773 of the wounded were treated for shock and anxiety and released. One hundred eighty-four Hezbollah fighters and 119 Israeli soldiers died in combat and the two kidnapped Israeli soldiers have yet to be released.[4]

In addition to the senseless wars and the tragic loss of life that has affected so many on both sides of the border, the Lebanese and Israelis also lack true statesmen capable of reversing this tragic trend, particularly since the assassination of Yitzhak Rabin in 1995. In their 2005 elections, both people thought they were voting in new leadership but got, instead, a rehash of the same old cast of characters, albeit in some cases sporting new clothes. These current leaders pursue the same failed policy of manufacturing wars for territorial gains and regional hegemony. Both Israel and Hezbollah willingly participate in a dangerous proxy war for the United States and Iran while the Siniora-Hariri-led Lebanese government takes orders from US Ambassador Jeffrey Feltman, a neo-con charged with carrying out President Bush's "democratization" of Lebanon. The losers in this high-stakes game of warfare are, of course, the Lebanese and Israeli people.

On a macrocosmic level, the repercussions are, however, far greater. While this book examines the tragedy in South Lebanon, it also addresses a critical question that ultimately affects us all. At what point should a government be held accountable for the consequences of its actions? If one regional power, Israel, can destroy large swaths of Lebanon at will, internally displace thirty percent of its population, indiscriminately bomb a defenseless civilian population, blanket entire regions with cluster bombs, cause an envi-

....

4   Human Rights Watch. "Why They Died: Civilian Casualties in Lebanon during the 2006 War." September 2007, Volume 19, No. 5(E). http://hrw.org/reports/2007/lebanon0907/

ronmental disaster the effects of which will last for generations, and suffer no consequences for its actions, is not the entire world ultimately endangered by such callous behavior? If the US government sanctions such actions, refuses to call for a cease-fire, provides Israel with jet fuel so that it can continue its bombing raids across Lebanon and insists in the final cease-fire resolution that Israel be absolved of any wrongdoing, should it not also be held accountable for its misguided actions, just as it insisted Saddam Hussein and Slobodan Milosevic be held accountable for their behavior? All wrongs, whether committed by the US or its allies, must be evaluated with the same criteria used to judge Hezbollah, Hamas and others. International law applies to not just a few powerless nations and resistance movements. If left unchecked, the actions of the United States and Israel will eventually erode a global mechanism that strives to maintain stability and security through a balance of power that is based on legitimacy and responsible behavior.

1

THE ORIGINS OF CHAOS

A year and a half after the July 2006 Hezbollah-Israeli war, Lebanon is on the verge of major civil unrest due in large part to the deep divide between Hezbollah, a Shiite movement, and the Sunni-led Siniora-Hariri government.

The crisis began in November 2006 when Hezbollah, politically emboldened after it withstood the Israeli Army's thirty-four day assault, walked out of the pro-American Siniora government. The pro-Syrian Hezbollah bloc demanded the formation of a new national-unity government in which the opposition would control one-third-plus-one seats, giving it veto power on such strategic issues as preserving its armed status and preventing Lebanon from falling into the US-Israeli orbit. Hezbollah accuses the Siniora government of collaboration with Israel and the United States.

Twelve months after the walk-out, with no apparent end to the bitter government stand-off, the infiltration of al-Qaeda-linked insurgents into a Palestinian refugee camp in the north and presidential elections originally scheduled for September 25, 2007 but postponed after twelve attempts until some time in early 2008, the Lebanese are in a state of panic, and rightly so. Lebanon has no functioning government because the Speaker of the House, Nabih Berri, who joined Hezbollah's boycott, refuses to call Parliament into session for anything other than choosing a new president but only if there is consensus ahead of time. Hezbollah spurns any attempt to force it to disarm, insisting Israel must first end its occupation of the Shebaa Farms in South Leb-

anon. The United Nations, at the request of the Siniora government, intends to initiate a tribunal to try those responsible for the
2005 assassination of Rafic Hariri; the pro-Syrian camp rejects
this American-backed scheme which, they believe, will find Syria
guilty regardless of the evidence. Maronite Christians, who tradi-
tionally choose Lebanon's president from their ranks, are bitterly
divided over which candidate to support. In a 105-day battle with
al-Qaeda-linked insurgents the Lebanese Army lost 165 soldiers.
In two separate incidents, sectarian violence between Sunnis and
Shiites has resulted in beheading and dismemberment. And last,
but no less serious, residents along the Lebanese-Israeli border
continue to feel powerless in the face of mounting threats. On a
daily basis Israel flies low-level incursions across their towns and
villages in violation of the fragile cease-fire that ended the thirty-
four-day war; Hezbollah continues to amass an impressive arsenal
of sophisticated weaponry, supplied by Iran; an attack by al-Qaeda-
linked terrorists killed six UN peacekeepers along the Israeli-Lebanese border and Washington continues to torpedo any possible
compromise between the Siniora government and Hezbollah.

Neither the opposition nor the government seems fazed by
this daunting list of crises. Instead of making the necessary concessions to save the country from further bloodshed and certain financial ruin, each camp, whether because of indifference,
intransigence or a willingness to play the role of political puppet
for a foreign power, continues to display a callous disregard for the
responsibilities with which they were charged – the well-being of
their nation and its people.

. . .

South Lebanon's continued descent into chaos has, to a large
degree, been fomented by foreign powers. The root cause of the
2006 Israeli-Hezbollah war can be traced back to the 1968 cross-
border skirmishes between the Palestinian Liberation Organization (PLO) and the Israeli Army. The PLO guerillas occupied villages
in South Lebanon from where they launched attacks into northern
Israel. The Israeli Army responded with reprisal raids, killing civil-

ians, destroying homes, crops and entire villages. A decade later, twenty-five thousand Israeli troops invaded South Lebanon to wipe out PLO guerillas who continued to lob Katyusha rockets across their border. The PLO evacuated the region ahead of the advancing Israeli troops leaving villagers to face a powerful military force unarmed. During the two-month siege five thousand innocent civilians were killed. In its 1982 invasion, which was intended to rid Lebanon of all Palestinian fighters, the Israeli Army killed ten thousand civilians in South Lebanon alone and created six hundred thousand refugees. Over the next eighteen years, Israel and its proxy, the South Lebanese Army, maintained a military occupation across a swath of South Lebanon that gave rise to a home-grown resistance movement called Hezbollah. While an organic part of Lebanon's Shiite community, representing forty percent of the overall population, Hezbollah is also loyal to the Shiite clerics in Iran who finance its organization and supply it with weaponry. More importantly, in the 2006 war, which the Arab world called the US-Iran proxy war, Hezbollah stood in for Iran. In the eyes of many Lebanese, Hezbollah is, therefore, both an inside and, by association, an outside player. Likewise, the same similarities exist within Israel, a country not only supported financially and supplied militarily by America, but heavily influenced by powerful political interest groups in Washington, D.C., who direct Israel's foreign policy toward its Arab neighbors. These policies are not always in Israel's best interest.

. . .

In ancient times indigenous Arabs and Jews shared this tiny speck of land along the Levant, an area we know today as South Lebanon and northern Israel. Together, they worked the lands, reaping equally of its rich bounty. Both communities were repeatedly besieged by invading armies. They were slaughtered, driven into exile or subjugated under foreign powers. Yet, in spite of these challenges, or perhaps because of them, they managed to live amicably as neighbors, often as close relatives through intermarriage. In large part, the success of their fellowship can be ascribed to leaders who recognized the need for solidarity over divisiveness and inter-communal conflicts, and knew how to encourage and nurture it.

Until 1948, when it fell under Israeli control, the northern reaches of the Upper Galilee included Tyre in South Lebanon. Flavius Josephus, the Roman historian, describes a great friendship between Hiram, the Phoenician King of Tyre, and Kings David and Solomon. The architect of the Temple of Jerusalem and of Solomon's two palaces, Hiram also supplied both the manpower and the wood from Lebanon's cedar trees to fashion the kings' elaborate edifices. According to Josephus, King Solomon paid Hiram a visit in Tyre and worshipped in one of his temples. Though Solomon already had several hundred wives, Hiram, in a gesture of friendship, offered him an additional bride – his youngest daughter. Tyrians possessed abundant ships; their sailors were skilled navigators and traders who controlled most of the Mediterranean trade. Solomon, for his part, had access to lucrative traffic routes in East Africa, Arabia and India. Together, the two kings forged commercial interests into a successful enterprise, the rewards of which they shared with their people.

After World War I, when the British and the French carved up the Ottoman Empire to create Lebanon, Syria, Palestine, Jordan, and Iraq, the idea of community was discarded for ideologies like Arab nationalism and Zionism. With power came self-interest and corruption. With imposed borders came disputes over land and resources, particularly water, a precious commodity in the Middle East.

Even in statehood Lebanon remained a collection of tribes with allegiance to their local leaders. As much as it tried over the years to become a harmonious multi-confessional society that successfully straddled both the Eastern and the newly-adopted Western cultures, it was, in reality, nothing of the sort. When the Lebanese most needed to come together as a nation under wise leadership with the common goal of surviving, they could not. Instead, each community looked to their tribal leaders for guidance. The result was civil war.

As a struggling new state, Israel faced similar difficulties. In the early 1900s, Eastern European Jews colonized Palestine with little regard for the native population. This was clearly Chaim Weizmann's thinking when he addressed the 1914 World Zionist Congress in Paris. Referring to Palestine, he called it "a land without people for a people without land," despite the fact that seven hundred thousand Arabs – Muslims and Christians – already lived there.

By the late 19th century, twenty thousand Jews had moved to Palestine to escape pogroms and rampant anti-Semitism in Russia and Romania. Following the abortive 1905 Russian revolution, a second wave of Jews immigrated to Palestine. Between 1900 and 1939 Jewish settlements in Palestine increased from twenty-two to two hundred. When the Ashkenazi, or white European Jews, declared themselves the elite class, thereby relegating the Maghrebi Jews from North Africa and the Sephardic Jews, those who settled in Arab communities after their expulsion from Spain in 1492, to second class status, Israel, too, became a fractured society. It had the added problem of an indigenous Palestinian population that would swell over the next sixty years from seven hundred thousand to five million.

In their rush to instill modernity along the Levant, the new leaders forgot the most important tool of governance – diplomacy. Hiram, David and Solomon understood its power and how important engaging and respecting the other was in resolving differences. Sadly, neither the Lebanese nor the Israeli leaders recognize that diplomacy secures cooperation and insures security and peace for their people. Confrontation, on the other hand, elicits only more warfare and misery.

For as long as leaders continue to invade and destroy each other's countries instead of finding common ground for compromise, the people of Lebanon and Israel are destined to endure more suffering. Unlike Israel, however, Lebanon, particularly in its current state of chaos, also risks partition. In the past two decades several countries that have fallen apart have done so painfully and amid extreme disorder. Such events wreak havoc on our global system of checks and balances and ultimately affect our entire world order. Yugoslavia divided into a half-dozen states. Bosnia later broke apart into two further entities – one Serbian Greek Orthodox and one combined Croatian Catholic and Bosnian Muslim. Serbia and Montenegro broke apart and Kosovo has recently followed.[5] The West Bank and Gaza are now ruled by two governments, Fatah and Hamas. Iraq will, in all likelihood, divide into Arab Sunni, Arab Shiite and Kurdish areas. If Lebanon's leaders cannot find common ground and elect a consensus president by early 2008, Lebanon risks following the same disastrous path. To survive as a nation, Lebanon's leaders must stop relying on their various international backers and begin, instead, to work as a team to settle differences. The US and the broader international community should be encouraging the various factions to come together to insure that the outcome of the upcoming presidential elections does not divide Lebanon. If, however, the US continues to meddle in Lebanon's internal politics and actively seeks to curtail any progress that does not fit into its scheme of "democratization," then a broader question begs to be asked. Is the partition of Lebanon the ultimate goal of the current American administration? A weakened Lebanon, with a pro-American president, would be forced into a peace treaty with Israel which seeks, by any means, the *de facto* annexation of South Lebanon and access to the Litani River water source. If such a plan succeeds, this would leave Israel the dominant player in the Middle East and reduce Lebanon and the already compliant Saudi Arabia, Jordan and Egypt to puppet regime status, thereby rubber-stamping all future US adventures in the region.

5   Amr, Hady. "Avoiding the Emergence of Two Lebanons." *Daily Star*, September 10, 2007.

2

WAR MEMORIES
OF MY OWN

On July 12, 2006, the day the Israeli-Hezbollah war began in South Lebanon, I was in San Antonio, Texas, at the invitation of the Gemini Ink Literary Center. I was conducting a workshop on writing memoirs, in part because of the success of my own memoir, *A Beirut Heart: One Woman's War*, an account of my experiences during the Lebanese civil war beginning in 1975.

I was not particularly alarmed when I heard on the morning news that Hezbollah had kidnapped two Israeli soldiers. To those of us who follow Lebanon closely, such abductions along the Israeli-Lebanese border, whether carried out by Israel or Hezbollah, are routine events. The kidnap victims are used as bargaining chips to negotiate the freedom of prisoners held by either side. Former Israeli Prime Minister Ariel Sharon negotiated with Hezbollah in January 2004, when he obtained the release of an Israeli colonel, a businessman and the remains of three soldiers, in exchange for thirty Lebanese and the remains of sixty others. When Sharon refused to release the rest of the agreed-upon prisoners, including a man held since 1978, Hassan Nasrallah, the Hezbollah leader, vowed to continue abducting Israeli soldiers.

However indefensible, I was convinced that Hezbollah's July 12 actions were just another unsettling episode in South Lebanon's tragic saga. I was wrong.

By evening, Lt. General Dan Halutz, the Israeli Chief of Staff, was warning that, "If the two Israeli soldiers are not returned, we will turn Lebanon's clock back twenty years,"[6] an obvious reference to the terrible destruction Lebanon suffered during its fifteen-year civil war. Israeli Prime Minister Ehud Olmert gave his own stern warning, saying, "The Lebanese government, of which Hezbollah is a part, is trying to undermine regional stability. Lebanon is responsible, and Lebanon will bear the consequences of its actions."[7] By the next day a widespread bombing campaign began.

Disheartened, I made my way back to my home in Eau Claire, Wisconsin. I could make no sense of Israel's disproportionate response, yet my trustworthy NPR reporters were in Beirut, in its southern suburbs and in South Lebanon, even in the north, telling me that Israeli war planes had just taken out the bridge near Ghazir, the one I had driven over a hundred times. An apartment building in East Beirut on Abdel Wahab Street had taken a direct hit. Many of my friends live on that street. The Lebanese Army barracks near Jamhour, my children's old school, took direct hits and eleven soldiers died.

The mention of Jamhour took me back to the morning I raced under the bombs in my VW Bug to rescue my children from school. In the early days of war a bridge north of Beirut was our only escape route. Now, bridges across the country were being systematically destroyed, preventing people from seeking safer refuge.

From the first days of the Israeli-Hezbollah war, I called Beirut several times a day, anxious for the safety of family and friends. I was curious, too, to hear the latest rumors, speculating as we did back in the '70s and early '80s about which foreign power would push for a cease-fire and when. I ran on adrenalin and my phone conversations seemingly gave me the fix I needed for the day.

....

6   CNN.com. November 25, 2006. http://edition.cnn.com/2006/WORLD/
     meast/07/12/mideast

7   Harel, Amos, Benn Aluf and Gideon Alon. "Government Okays Massive Strikes on
     Lebanon." *Haaretz*, 13 July 2006.

Though nights in Eau Claire, Wisconsin are peaceful, I found myself waking up emotionally exhausted. I burst into tears when someone asked about our family in Beirut. I reverted to being a news junkie, listening to NPR, watching CNN and surfing the web between the *Daily Star* in Beirut, the *Independent* in London and *Haaretz* in Israel.

As I watched the devastating scenes, I realized that my daily struggles for survival during the civil war were, by comparison, trivial. Then, I had only to deal with such things as water shortages and power outages. I feared car bombs when I walked the streets of my neighborhood, a far cry from aerial bombing raids, which targeted civilians as they fled their homes. Dozens of fresh corpses turned up daily in every corner of the city; in the summer of 2006, the numbers were in the hundreds each week.

During the civil war, my physician husband, Michel, had a fully functioning hospital to treat wounded civilians. In July 2006 doctors in South Lebanon had to administer medical care from makeshift clinics with little or no medication or equipment to tens of thousands of victims. In '82, any time Israeli warplanes bombed the nearby Palestinian camps, a hammer pounded relentlessly inside my head. Though my body convulsed as if in concert with each bomb that battered the ground, then exploded, I never feared for my life. During the 2006 bombing raids, people's homes in the south and in Beirut's southern suburb were indiscriminately leveled on top of them. The smell of their decomposing bodies hung in the stifling summer air for days. Once you have had that smell in your nostrils your mind keeps an olfactory memory of it for the rest of your life.

. . .

In July and August 2006, the people of South Lebanon subsisted in ways I could hardly fathom. They had no water for simple household chores, not even drinking water for their children. Out of desperation, they resorted to using sewage and waste water polluted by phosphorus bombs. Some eight hundred thousand were now homeless and if their houses somehow managed to resist the bombing raids, they also had no electricity. Many in the south are too poor to own a car. They had no money to hire a taxi to usher their family to safety. If they had transportation and fuel, they feared traveling the few remaining routes out of the south because the Israeli Army refused to guarantee anyone safe passage, even Red Cross ambulances.

· · ·

One such eyewitness account by an ambulance driver, Red Cross volunteer Nader Joudi, vividly depicts just how difficult it was to transport the injured to the hospital.

At the Red Cross office in Tyre, three volunteer medics dressed in their orange overalls and got into their ambulance. The plan was to drive halfway, meet the local ambulance and transfer the three patients to their vehicle to return to Tyre.

The ambulance headlamps were on, the blue light overhead was flashing, and another light illuminated the Red Cross flag when the first Israeli missile hit, shearing off the right leg of the man on the stretcher inside. As he lay screaming beneath fire and smoke, ambulance workers scrambled for safety, crawling over glass in the dark. Then another missile hit the second ambulance.

We stopped the ambulances for barely two minutes. We loaded two patients into the vehicle: Ahmed, who had been hit by shrapnel in his stomach, and his fourteen-year-old son, Mohammad. We were just easing Ahmed's eighty-year-old mother who was severely wounded inside the ambulance and setting up a saline drip when the missile struck. I had to abandon Ahmed to rush the old woman and child inside to safety. There was no way I could reach Ahmed. It was horrible. He was screaming and we couldn't do anything.

As the Red Cross volunteers radioed for help another missile plunged through the roof of the second ambulance.

By the time patients and the ambulance crew reached Tyre, Ahmed was unconscious after losing one leg and suffering several fractures to the other.

His son had lost part of his foot and his mother was dead, her body riddled with shrapnel. The three Red Cross volunteers suffered shrapnel wounds to their arms, faces and legs.

The Lebanese Red Cross, whose ambulance service for South Lebanon is run entirely by volunteers, immediately announced it would cease all rescue missions unless Israel guaranteed their safety through the United Nations or the International Red Cross.[8]

· · ·

While death and dying was a constant in South Lebanon, life in northern Israel was no less intense for a population with little or no experience living under a rain of Katyusha rockets. According to David, a resident of Kiryat Shmona in northern Israel:

We did everything in fear when the war started. We ate in fear. We sat at home in fear and we showered in fear. But at least I am still alive to tell you my story.

Twenty-four thousand people live in Kiryat Shmona. Every one fled except for some six thousand residents. We lost several homes to Katyusha rockets. Our firefighters have had to battle several forest fires and our high school has been hit three times by rockets.

I feel very lucky though compared to what my sister has endured. She lives in Acre, also in northern Israel. Shimon, her husband, and her fifteen-year-old daughter, Mazal, were killed and her seventeen-year-old son, Raz, suffered shrapnel wounds. I talked to her shortly after the tragedy. According to her the siren sounded and everyone ran to the nearby shelter. When the rockets stopped falling, Shimon and Mazal and others went outside to see what had happened. Within minutes, more rockets landed. One of them hit Shimon and Mazal. Their bodies were terribly damaged but they were holding hands. That's an image I just can't get out of my head so you can imagine how difficult it is for my sister.

I hate this war, any war. It's always a tragedy whether you're Jewish or

....

8   Goldenberg, Suzanne. "Red Cross Ambulances Destroyed in Israeli Air Strike on Rescue Mission." *The Guardian*, July 25, 2006.

Arab. Every thinking person here knows that we are no different from the Arabs. We have the same bloodlines.

Leaders, no matter whether they are Nasrallah or Olmert, they are all alike. They make decisions away from the people without ever consulting them. Their people don't count. It is their agenda that counts. And the leaders don't give a damn that in war it is the people who suffer. Wasn't there a time in history when diplomacy was the first line of defense?[9]

. . .

An optimist will assume that after exhausting every other possibility, the next American administration will remember that diplomacy secures cooperation even from its staunched enemies and ultimately insures world stability. More realistically, it will be the catastrophe in Iraq, a belligerent and powerful Iran, instability in Saudi Arabia, Egypt, and Jordan and the possibility that other players, particularly China and India, will gain influence in the Middle East that will finally convince the United States that a different strategy is urgently needed. America has an historical opportunity to defuse the broader risks of mass destruction across the Middle East by offering all adversaries a place at the negotiating table. Should such an invitation be extended, everyone would accept.

---

9   Author interviewed David by phone from his home in Kiryat Shmona on May 23, 2007.

3

SOUTH LEBANON
AND GAZA:
TWO FAILED POLICIES

The similarities between Israel and Lebanon and their people are not limited to war and poor leadership. Other parallels are even more striking. The tragedy of South Lebanon is a mirror image of the Gaza Strip, a place also devastated by military incursions. Each place is defined by a specific leader and his movement. Hezbollah is the non-state actor in Lebanon; Hamas plays a similar role in Israel/Palestine. Hassan Nasrallah, an Iranian-schooled Shiite cleric, is spiritual, political and military leader of Hezbollah. The Sunni-Hamas leader, Ismail Haniyeh, is Prime Minister of the Palestinian Authority. Each leader belongs to a weak, ineffectual and corrupt government. Though it is currently boycotting the government, the Hezbollah bloc holds six ministerial posts in the Lebanese cabinet and fifty-five out of 128 seats in Parliament. Hamas won seventy-six out of 132 seats in the democratically held elections that the United States insisted the Palestinians hold in January 2006.

In the present Lebanese standoff, Hezbollah refuses to recognize the constitutionality of the Siniora-Hariri government. In Gaza, Hamas, for its part, will only recognize a State of Israel within its pre-'67 border. While one group is Shiite, the other Sunni, both have the backing of Syria and Iran, while the US and

Israel back both Palestinian President Mahmoud Abbas and Lebanon's Siniora-Hariri government.

During the summer of 2006 Israel conducted two wars simultaneously, one in Lebanon to crush Hezbollah, the other in Gaza to destroy Hamas. Both were sanctioned by the Bush administration.

Israel's response to the kidnapping of its two soldiers in Lebanon was twofold: a massive aerial bombing campaign against Hezbollah strongholds and the deliberate destruction of Lebanon's infrastructure. Israel's goal was to clear the border area south of the Litani River, a vital water source that Israeli covets. To succeed, Israel needed to destroy as many villages as possible. I cite Qana as an example. It was bombed eighty times, each bombing raid systematically destroying as many buildings as possible.

And the two kidnapped soldiers? As of this writing, the Israeli government has still not made an attempt to negotiate their release.

On June 23, 2006, nineteen days before the Lebanon war, Israeli troops crossed into Gaza and kidnapped a Palestinian physician and his young nephew. On June 25 Palestinian militants retaliated with a raid on Israeli military positions near Gaza, killing two soldiers and capturing one, Captain Gilad Shalit. No attempt was made to negotiate the release of the Israeli soldier. Instead, on June 27 Israel launched a large scale military assault on Gaza, destroying bridges and a power plant which plunged most of Gaza into darkness. The goal was to protect the Israeli border town of Sderot in the Negev. It became home to poor Jewish immigrants in the early 1950s, a few years after it had been cleared of Palestinians living in what was then the village of Najd. Since 2001 more than forty-five hundred Kassam rockets have landed in Sderot, killing seven residents and injuring dozens.[10]

. . .

....

10 "Israelis Traumatized in Sderot." *Sydney Morning Herald*, May 20, 2007. www.smh.com.au.news

What is the Gaza Strip and why are events there so relevant to the situation in South Lebanon? Once again, there are similarities.

The Gaza Strip, an area one-eighth the size of Rhode Island, represents one percent of historic Palestine. The Strip is approximately twenty-five miles long and seven miles wide, and is home to 1.4 million Palestinians.

In August 2005 then-Prime Minister Ariel Sharon carried out what he called a "unilateral disengagement" from the Gaza Strip ("unilateral" means that he acted without prior consultation with the Palestinian Authority), pulling out seven thousand eight hundred Israeli settlers who occupied the Strip for thirty-eight years. They comprised one half of one percent of the population in Gaza, yet they occupied twenty percent of the land. An additional ten percent was under Israeli military control.

The Palestinian economy was for the most part agricultural. After their lands were confiscated and their orchards uprooted to make way for Israeli settlements, Palestinians were obliged to become day laborers inside Israel. When former Prime Ministers Barak and Sharon closed off Gaza and the West Bank from Israel for long periods of time, denying Palestinians the right to enter, Palestinians suddenly found themselves without work and without money, unable to feed their families. According to the World Bank, eighty-six percent of Gazan households depend on food relief from the UN or other humanitarian agencies.

During Israel's thirty-eight-year occupation of Gaza, Palestinians were not allowed to build a seaport along the Mediterranean to export their goods. Similarly, they were forbidden to reconstruct an old, abandoned airport. Unless the Israeli government reverses these decisions Palestinians will remain without a seaport or airport. Since the only way in and out of Gaza into Israel is through the Eretz checkpoint manned by Israeli soldiers, Israel will still be able to cut off the supply of food and medicine, raw materials, water, fuel, gas, and electricity at will. Gazans are still feeling the effects of the June 2006 attack on their electricity plant. A year later some fifty thousand people are still without power and former Israeli Prime Minister Netanyahu has proposed cutting water and electricity to all of Gaza.

After the Israeli withdrawal the Palestinian Authority had plans to revitalize the Palestinian economy in the Gaza Strip, where unemployment reached almost ninety percent in some areas, by encouraging investment and creating jobs. In order to accomplish this, Israel's cooperation was needed. However, almost two years later, with Gaza surrounded by concrete walls and high fencing, Israel still strictly controls all access in and out of the strip, including the Rafah Crossing between Gaza and Egypt, for both people and goods. With absolute control still firmly in the hands of the Israelis, the Gaza Strip is cut off from the West Bank and from the rest of the world.

James D. Wolfensohn was President of the World Bank from 1995 to 2005 before becoming Middle East Envoy for the Quartet (the US, Russia, the European Union and the UN) in May 2005. He was tasked with monitoring the Israeli disengagement from Gaza and helping to heal the ailing Palestinian economy. He successfully raised $9 billion toward that effort. In November 2005, three months after Israel withdrew its settlers from the Gaza Strip, he acted as mediator between Israel and the PA in the negotiation of transit routes for goods to and from Gaza. He also donated money of his own to help the Palestinians buy Israeli-owned greenhouses in Gaza. Both US administration interference and the rise of Hamas to power and the subsequent boycott combined to derail his mission.[11] A frustrated Wolfensohn returned to the US in April 2006. It was not until July 2007 when Hamas took control of Gaza that he felt compelled to speak on the record:

"Part of the reason the slide into violence happened, in my view, is that the conditions in Gaza deteriorated so terribly. If you recall, in the time of the withdrawal in 2005 there was a day or two of people looting but within forty-eight hours it was under con-

....

[11] Smooha, Sharar. "All the Dreams We Had Are Now Gone." *Haaretz*, July 19, 2007. Accessed September 24, 2007. http://www.haaretz.com/hasen/spages/884018.html

trol. Things were peaceful in Gaza and this was not because of an Israeli military presence. It was because the Palestinians recognized that if they wanted to have any hope, they needed to be in a more peaceful mode. I remember seeing the greenhouses while touring Gaza with Mahmoud Abbas and looking at the fruits and everything. There was a joyous atmosphere: 'Boy, we're about to get this going and we're going to have hotels by the beaches and we're going to have tourism and it's going to be fantastic, and the Palestinians really know how to be hosts.' But in the months afterwards, first of all Sharon became ill, then Olmert was elected and then there was a clear change of attitude.

"At the same time powerful forces in the US administration worked behind my back. They did not believe in the border terminals agreement between Gaza and the West Bank and wanted to undermine my status as the Quartet emissary. The official who tore apart every aspect of the terminals agreement was Elliott Abrams, the neoconservative who was appointed Deputy National Security advisor in charge of disseminating democracy in the Middle East."[12]

Currently, Palestinians need Israeli permits to travel within the occupied West Bank, between the West Bank and Gaza, and into Israel. Palestinians living in Gaza need Israeli permission to leave Gaza at the Rafah Crossing which exits into Egypt. During the month of May 2007, the crossing was open four days. In July 2007 an estimated five thousand people were waiting to cross on either side of the Rafah Crossing.

On May 16, 2007, Israel renewed air strikes on the Gaza Strip, firing on a Hamas Executive Support Forces base in southern Gaza. Over the next two days, according to the Palestinian Centre for Human Rights (PCHR), Israel intensified air attacks targeting civilian facilities. Israel says these attacks came in response to the launching of homemade rockets at Sderot. During this period Pal-

....

12   Ibid.

estinian guerrillas did, in fact, continue to launch Kassam rockets into Sderot, killing two and injuring several others, bringing the number of deaths to nine since 2001.

According to PCHR, a May 20 Israeli air strike on the Gaza home of a Hamas politician killed seven members of his family and three other civilians. This latest operation in Gaza came in the midst of a week of fighting between Palestinian groups that claimed about fifty lives and news that the Bush administration intended to increase its funding and arming of the forces loyal to Mohammad Dahlan, President Abbas's security chief in the Gaza Strip, as part of a plan developed by US Deputy National Security Advisor Elliott Abrams to violently overthrow the democratically-elected Hamas government.[13] According to European observers the US was grooming Dahlan to eventually assume the presidency and restore Fatah to power.[14] However, many in Fatah are uncomfortable with Dahlan's and Abbas's cooperation with the US and Israel and advocate cooperation, instead, between Fatah and Hamas.

The main cause of tension in Gaza has been over who controls the Palestinian security services and how efficient these services are. Additional factors complicate matters: a multitude of armed rogue splinter groups has emerged since June 2006, making violence almost impossible to contain. Israel, in its effort to destroy Hamas, has separated Gaza from the West Bank and isolated it almost completely from the rest of the world while Islamic Jihad, which refuses to abide by Hamas's cease-fire with Israel, continues to fire Kassam rockets into Sderot.

Since his election in January 2006, Hamas leader Ismail Haniyeh has maintained his cease-fire agreement with Israel. In May 2007 he offered a ten-year truce with Israel in exchange for Isra-

....

13 Khatib, Ghassan. "A Complication of Adverse Conditions." May 21, 2007. www.bitterlemons.org

14 Crooke, Alastair. "Our Second Biggest Mistake in the Middle East." *London Review of Books*, Volume 29, No. 13, July 5, 2007.

el's agreement to end the siege of Gaza and the West Bank. Israel did not respond to this offer.

Violence erupted in Gaza on June 14, 2007 between Hamas and Fatah when Hamas forcibly removed Mohammad Dahlan's security forces from Gaza. Abbas then dismissed the government and declared the formation of an emergency government, thereby bringing to an end what remained of Palestinian unity.

With Hamas in control of Gaza, both the US and the Israeli government have pledged to support Abbas's Fatah. As a gesture of "good will," Israel plans to ease roadblocks and security restrictions and release approximately $80 million of the funds it has withheld from the Palestinian Authority since January 2006 when Hamas won in the Palestinian elections. As a result, hundreds of thousands of workers have gone without a paycheck for the past year and a half. Israel and the US also plan to isolate Gaza. As of July 16, 2007, the US forbade both Western Union and DHL from transferring any money into the Gaza Strip.

According to US Secretary of State Envoy to the Middle East, David Welch, "We are supporting the legitimate security forces and enhancing them in order to establish a Palestinian entity which will be able to provide security and stability for Palestinian citizens, and we will be committed to this in the future."[15]

In a leaked report in June 2007, retired UN Special Envoy to the Middle East Alvaro De Soto contradicts Mr. Welch's statement, saying, "The Americans clearly encouraged a confrontation between Fatah and Hamas and worked to isolate and damage Hamas and built up Fatah with recognition and weaponry."[16]

In contrast to the Gaza siege, which is entering into its second year, the Hezbollah-Israel war lasted only thirty-four days. However, the political crisis between Sunnis and Shiites and the

....

15   Rizk, Philip. "The Failing of Gaza." *CounterPunch*, June 28, 2007.
     www.counterpunch.org/rizko6282007.html

16   Ibid. Also: Black, Ian. "UN Envoy: Anti-Hamas Rhetoric Undermines
     Democracy." *Guardian Unlimited*, June 13, 2007. www.guardian.co.uk/print

intense three week battle in May 2007 between Fatah al-Islam and the Lebanese Army inside a Palestinian camp in northern Lebanon suggests yet another major crisis brewing, this time with some familiar outside players – the Bush administration and its Deputy National Security Advisor, Elliott Abrams, the same person in charge of funding and arming President Abbas against Hamas.

The idea behind the plan in Lebanon was to covertly fund the Sunni, al-Qaeda-like Fatah al-Islam as a counterweight to Hezbollah. If any of this sounds familiar, it is. America's CIA recruited and trained al-Qaeda insurgents as a counterweight to the Russian Army in Afghanistan in the late '70s. When they successfully expelled the Russians with the help of their CIA-trained fighters, the Americans packed up, went home and seemingly forgot about the thousands of Islamic militants they left behind who were well-equipped, motivated by religious fervor and primed to attack the next foreign power that thought to invade a Middle East country.

The irony here is that Israel did the very same thing. It encouraged the rise of Hamas as a counterweight to the PLO, the secular coalition composed of Fatah and various other nationalist movements. Hamas, which means Islamic Resistance Movement, was founded in 1987 by Sheikh Ahmed Yassin, a man who spent years in Israeli prisons. It was then-Prime Minister Menachem Begin who assisted Yassin's start-up of a "humanitarian" organization known as the Islamic Association of Mujama in 1978. The roots of this Islamist group are in the fundamentalist Muslim Brotherhood, of which Hamas is an offshoot. Begin and his right-wing strategists devised the theory of creating Hamas as an alternative to Fatah because they believed that Muslim Brotherhood types would devote themselves to charity and religious study and passively accept the occupation.[17]

After Sheikh Yassin was released from prison and began organizing his movement, he was allowed to publicly call for the

....

17 Rosenberg, MJ. "A Hamas Run Gaza: We Can Thank Ourselves." *Israeli Policy Forum*, Friday, Volume 327, June 15, 2007.

destruction of the State of Israel by force of arms. However, when Mubarak Awad, a Christian Palestinian peace activist, advocated the use of Ghandi-like resistance to the Israeli occupation, he was seized by the Israeli Army and forcibly expelled from Israel. Until 1993, US officials in the Consular Office in Jerusalem met with Hamas leaders but refused to meet with anyone from the PLO. This despite the fact that the PLO had renounced terrorism and had unilaterally recognized Israel as far back as 1988.[18]

When Hamas captured a majority of Parliament in the January 2006 elections with only forty-four percent of the vote, it had the right to select the prime minister and form a new government. Another irony is that the position of prime minister did not exist under the original constitution of the Palestinian Authority but was added in March 2003 at the insistence of the US, which desired a counterweight to Yasser Arafat. As a result, while the elections allowed Abbas to retain the presidency, he was forced to share power with Ismail Haniyeh, the Hamas Prime Minister.[19] However, the West imposed financial sanctions on the Hamas government and isolated it politically. Instead of helping Fatah through the transition and facilitating Palestinian unity, and taking advantage of a real chance to include Hamas, the international community, and in particular the US, pursued an aggressive policy of internal division thereby establishing the conditions for havoc in Gaza.[20]

As of July 14, 2007, Israel still insisted it would maintain its complete ban on aid or have any contact with the Gaza Strip until Hamas recognizes Israel's right to exist, a condition neither Jordan nor Egypt had to agree to in advance of negotiations.[21]

Since a policy of punishment encourages radicals to gain a foot-

....

18 Zunes, Stephen. "The Rise of Hamas." *Foreign Policy in Focus*, June 26, 2007.

19 Ibid.

20 Crooke, Alastair. "Our Second Biggest Mistake in the Middle East." *London Review of Books*, Volume 29, No. 13, July 5, 2007.

21 Rosenberg, MJ. "Palestinians First." *Israeli Policy Forum*, Friday, Issue #325, June 1, 2007. www.ipforum.org

hold in Gaza why then is it not in Israel's best interest to end the siege, thereby weakening the appeal of al-Qaeda-like insurgents, the likes of whom have already appeared in Lebanon?

Until all responsible parties agree to reverse their failed policies, tragedies like South Lebanon and Gaza will continue to repeat themselves. Israel, for its part, bears responsibility for Gaza's terrible humanitarian crisis and for its repeated invasions and ultimate destruction of South Lebanon. Hamas, after it won elections in January 2006, had a duty to the Palestinian people to behave responsibly and it did not. Instead of reigning in violence, it allowed it to continue. Instead of addressing the needs of its people and assuming responsible leadership roles, it stubbornly refused to make any concessions. As a result, it forfeited needed international aid and support, squandering not only the fruit of its victory but any chance for the Palestinian people to realize peace and security.[22]

Hezbollah, for its part, must be held accountable for its role in the devastating 2006 war that tore apart Lebanon and northern Israel and for its unwillingness to make the necessary compromises with its equally obstinate Lebanese partners to ward off further civil unrest.

Peace requires compromises and the political will to make it happen. Alas, unlike the indigenous Arabs and Jews of ancient times who shared this land, the Lebanese and Israelis are a long way from realizing this worthy goal.

....

22 Zogby, James J. "Self-Inflicted Deadly Wounds." *The Jordan Times*, May 29, 2007.

4

THE JULY WAR

On Wednesday, July 12, 2006, the first day of the Israeli-Hezbollah war, *Haaretz*, in its Internet edition, reported that in a sharp departure from Israel's response to previous Hezbollah attacks, the cabinet session unanimously agreed that the Lebanese government should be held responsible for the kidnapping of Israeli soldiers.[23]

By 9:50 P.M. on July 12 the Israeli Air Force had already bombed bridges in central Lebanon and in the south. In those initial attacks, according to Amnesty International, some forty Lebanese civilians were killed near Nabatiya, including a family of ten, eight of whom were children; near Tyre a family of seven was killed.[24]

Shortly after the first Israeli attack on Lebanon on Wednesday evening, July 12, Hezbollah started its rocket attack on northern Israel. The Israeli government knew right from the start that launching its offensive would expose the residents of northern Israel to heavy Katyusha rocket attacks. According to Tanya Reinhart, this was openly discussed at the first government meeting following the kidnapping. One cannot avoid the conclusion that for the Israeli Army and government, endangering the lives of res-

....

23   Reinhart, Tanya. "Burning Lebanon, Israel's New Middle East." *CounterPunch*, July 27, 2006. http://counterpunch.org/reinhart07272006.html

24   Ibid.

idents of northern Israel was a price worth paying in order to justify the planned offensive.[25]

Hassan Nasrallah, at least during the initial days of the conflict, offered to stop bombing northern Israel if the Israeli Army halted its assault on Lebanon. President Bush, meanwhile, refused to join the international calls for a prompt ceasefire. Instead, he unconditionally defended Israel's bombing of Lebanon and claimed that Syria should be held accountable for fostering terrorism.[26]

Late in the evening of July 12, Israel launched its first attack on Beirut. It bombed the city's international airport, killing twenty-seven civilians. In response Hezbollah's rocket attacks intensified on Thursday, July 13, when more than one hundred Katyusha rockets were fired into Israel in the largest attack of its sort since the 1982 Lebanon War. Two Israeli civilians were killed in this attack and 132 were taken to the hospital. When Israel started destroying the Shiite neighborhoods in southern Beirut on July 14, Hezbollah extended its rocket attacks to Haifa.[27]

. . .

What was it like to be in Haifa under a hail of rockets? I spoke by phone with two women, each with a different reaction.

My name is Abir. I am thirty-two-years-old and I live in Haifa in northern Israel. I am Palestinian. The Israeli government refers to me as an Arab Israeli but my family has been in Galilee for generations, before the State of Israel, so I am Palestinian. The majority of Palestinians live in northern Israel in the Galilee. Haifa itself is about twenty-four percent Palestinian.

The war with Hezbollah was very difficult for many reasons. I was afraid for myself, and of course, for my family and friends. I could see from my apartment where the rockets were falling. My roommate and I spent

25   Ibid.

26   Lin, Sharat G. "Who Started It? Chronology of the Latest Crisis in the Middle East." *CounterPunch*, July 25, 2006. http://www.counterpunch.org/lin07252006. html

27   Reinhardt, Tanya.

our nights listening to the war and crying. We felt like we were in a state of perpetual mourning.

My roommate and I could have gone into the shelter in our building but chose not to since it was a privilege many Palestinians didn't have. Hezbollah's rockets fell on both Arab villages and on mixed neighborhoods, so no one was immune. It appeared that Hezbollah was mainly targeting strategic places like the huge military base in Haifa and the military traffic control center in Miron in northern Israel. Near Miron, there is also another military base built right alongside a Palestinian secondary school. So, again, no one was immune.

In the mixed cities like Haifa, there are neighborhoods that are seventy percent Palestinian but with only one shelter for two thousand people. Some Arab villages have shelters but certainly not enough. Too often the local councils simply decided to spend the money allocated for shelters on something else.

Another reason I stayed away from the shelters was because I didn't want to be stuck with Jewish Israelis. The racism and fascism in Haifa during the war against Palestinians was unbearable. In normal times it is difficult to be Palestinian in Israel, even though I am a citizen of the State of Israel, but during the war it took all my inner strength to stay calm. The general comments ran something like this: "Too bad Hezbollah isn't sending all the bombs on your neighborhoods so we can be rid of you." This was particularly painful to hear because I work against racism in Israel and this war in a few days ruined everything I and others have been working hard to change. The NGO I work with is called Mossawa, which in Arabic means "equality." Its mission is to end racism and achieve equal rights for the 1.3 million Arab citizens in Israel.

The only way I could spend some of my pent-up energy during the war was to go out and protest. I joined the thousands of Israelis and Palestinians who marched in the streets of Haifa protesting the Israeli government's disproportionate response to Hezbollah rockets. No, I am not contradicting myself. While some Jewish Israelis were extremely hostile to us, there were thousands who felt as I did and were not afraid to protest the Israeli government openly. Thousands of Jewish Israelis also marched in Tel Aviv.

By the way, my roommate is Israeli. Her name is Hanna. We're both activists trying to improve relations between Israelis and Palestinians. We spent our days, when not protesting in the streets, escorting foreign journalists around Haifa. Israel's Foreign Ministry set up its press conference in the same hotel the foreign journalists were staying in so we felt it was necessary to give these journalists other points of view and to let them talk to people other than those designated by the Israeli government. As you may know, in a war situation, Israel imposes strict censorship on news coverage. I believe you had the same thing in the beginning of the Iraq war except those journalists were embedded.

The Israeli press said the government was justified in sending rockets into South Lebanon because it was defending the sovereignty of the state and protecting its citizens. We tried to tell the foreign journalists that the Israeli military was no different than Hezbollah in endangering civilian lives. Here, too, many journalists toe the official line when Israel goes into combat mode. There is an enemy outside that is threatening Israel and everyone must stand united. Protesting, in their eyes, is giving support to the enemy.

I was arrested during one of the demonstrations because I was escorting foreign journalists. The police put me in a car for an hour, then drove me to the police station cursing me the entire time. Of course I kept my mouth shut so as not to get into more trouble. I was released a few hours later but put under house arrest for five days. My roommate received much harsher treatment at the hands of the police because she is Jewish and Jews are supposed to stick together to support their government.

Many Israelis were upset at how poorly the army performed against Hezbollah. For their defense, I do not think they knew to what extent people were killed in South Lebanon or how difficult this type of war is to fight. If they depended only on Israeli news, they certainly did not see the massacres, like the one in Qana. I knew what was going on because I have satellite television. Israel is a very militaristic society and it is extremely hard for Israelis to see someone other than themselves win in a battle. In fact, this is the first time someone has stood up to the Israeli Army. Of course they also have the complex of the persecuted and this too is normal given the trauma of the Holocaust.

I cannot pass judgment on Hezbollah because I am not Lebanese. On the other hand, I condemn Olmert for going to war as a first option. Recently, there was a stand-off between Iran and Great Britain over the kidnapping of British sailors off the Iranian coast. Quiet diplomacy was initiated, the men were released and war was averted. Why couldn't Olmert have done the same thing with Hezbollah, particularly when his predecessor, Ariel Sharon, had already set a precedent of negotiating with Hezbollah over Lebanese and Israeli prisoners abducted along the border?[28]

. . .

Marion is a sixty-year-old Jewish Israeli who lives in Haifa.

If I had gone to work the day a Hezbollah rocket hit my office, I would not be alive today and talking to you on the phone. The entire ceiling to floor wall next to my desk is glass. When the rocket hit, the glass completely shattered. Huge sharp-edged pieces fell onto my desk. When I saw the mess in my office the day after the attack, I broke down and cried. I was very lucky.

But now I am very angry.

I don't think [former Prime Minister] Ehud Barak should have pulled our troops out of Lebanon in May 2000 without destroying Hezbollah once and for all. He was a coward bowing to public pressure to bring our troops home. He also put our soldiers in a difficult position. Do you realize that Israel has always stood up to the Arab enemy and by pulling our troops out of Lebanon, under cover of night I might add, Barak appeared to have given a victory to Hezbollah. This emboldened them to the extent that they thought they could defeat us.

Just look at all the arms they have now, all supplied by Iran, a country that wants to wipe us off the face of the map. Frankly, I was surprised when Sharon agreed to negotiate with these terrorists back in 2004. I understand the only reason he did it was because the captured Israeli businessman was an acquaintance of his. That kind of horse-trading with the enemy was so atypical of Ariel Sharon. He set a terrible precedent, one that Hezbollah thought it could take advantage of.

....

28 Author conducted this interview via telephone on May 25, 2007 with Abir in Haifa.

Olmert has my vote of confidence. If he has to bomb all of Lebanon to destroy Hezbollah, so be it. We have suffered at the hands of the Palestinians for far too long. We should not have to also suffer rocket attacks from Hezbollah.[29]

. . .

In the first seventy-two hours of the war, Hezbollah's primary arsenals were targeted by the Israeli Air Force (IAF). Israeli commanders had identified these bunkers through signal intercepts from Hezbollah communications, satellite-reconnaissance, photos from drone aircraft and from a network of trusted-human sources recruited by Israeli intelligence officers living in South Lebanon, including a large number of foreign nationals registered as guest workers. Despite an intense bombing campaign, the attacks on Hezbollah positions failed. According to one US official who observed the war closely, the IAF's offensive degraded perhaps only seven percent of the total military resource assets. In his opinion, Israeli air strikes across the south and in Beirut's southern neighborhood were absolutely futile.[30]

. . .

Timur Goksel, Senior Advisor and Official Spokesman for the United Nations Interim Force in Lebanon (UNIFIL) weighs in with his assessment of the Israeli bombing campaign:

"The idea behind causing such horrific damage to civilian infrastructure was to convince the population to turn on Hezbollah. In practice, the opposite happened. After the attacks there was disquiet among groups in Lebanon about Hezbollah's kidnapping of the Israeli soldier. Now people are shocked and enraged that

....

29 Author conducted this interview via telephone on May 25, 2007 with Marion in Haifa.

30 Crooke, Alastair and Mark Perry. "How Hezbollah Defeated Israel. Part One: Winning the Intelligence War." *Conflicts Forum*. http://conflictsforum.org/cf-publications/articles-series

the US has given the green light to destroy their country. They're shocked to think that their friends – the US, France, Saudi Arabia – are colluding with Israel to destroy Lebanon.

"I think Hezbollah also miscalculated. Nasrallah thinks very carefully about the consequences of his actions before he acts. Usually it's a checklist: how will the action affect Hezbollah, then Syria, then Iran. This time he changed the rules of the game.

"As for Israel, its claim that it destroyed most of Hezbollah's weapons is based on a false premise. Hezbollah isn't keeping Katyusha rockets and missiles in houses. They have weapons depots for these in deep bunkers. For two years I watched Hezbollah move back their missiles from the border area. The air strikes haven't taken out the weapons as claimed. Hezbollah is still firing an average of ninety rockets a day. And I know they can continue firing at that level for several months without re-supplying.

"I have been in countless hours of meetings with some of the Hezbollah leaders. I can guarantee that they would have welcomed a quiet dialogue with the United States. We don't do our fundamental homework anymore. You've got to empathize with the enemy to the extent that you don't see your enemy as a cartoon character but someone who might be smarter than anybody in your administration."[31]

. . .

On July 14 Lebanon asked for an emergency meeting at the UN Security Council to discuss the possibility of a UN-mandated comprehensive cease-fire and the lifting of the Israeli air and sea blockades of Lebanon. US Ambassador to the United Nations John Bolton refused to urge restraint from Israel and instead blamed Syria and Iran for the current crisis.[32]

By July 15 Israel had bombed bridges and roads in South Leba-

....

31 Goksel, Timur. Interviewed by Kevin Sites. "The Great Game." August 3, 2006. hotzone.yahoo.com.

32 Crooke, Alastair and Mark Perry.

non, dividing the country and stranding hundreds of thousands of civilians desperate to flee the combat zone.

On July 16 the IAF hit Sidon, Nabatiya, Baalbeck, even as far north as Tripoli, killing scores of civilians. In Beirut's southern Shiite neighborhood of Dahiyeh, Israel used US-made GBU-28 guided bunker buster bombs in an attempt to destroy Hezbollah's underground bunkers. Dozens of twelve- to fifteen-story buildings completely collapsed into mountains of rubble. The strikes continued, leveling large areas of Beirut. Just south of the city, Israel bombed Jiyyeh, a large power plant, leaving the region without electricity. The cumulative death toll after just four days of bombing climbed to 160.[33]

Meanwhile, in Haifa, a Hezbollah rocket attack killed eight people. Other rockets hit Tiberias, Nazareth, Aula, Give Ela and a settlement in the Israeli-occupied Golan Heights. The cumulative death toll in Israel reached twenty-four: twelve civilians and twelve military.[34]

. . .

On July 20 the US Marines began evacuating American citizens via amphibious landing craft from a beach north of Beirut before ferrying them to Cyprus. Similar rescue missions were conducted near Tyre. Meanwhile, diplomatic efforts got under way to discuss deploying a UN or NATO peacekeeping force as a buffer between Israeli and Hezbollah forces along the Israeli-Lebanese border.[35]

. . .

One of the people evacuated, a Lebanese American, lives in southern Wisconsin. Her first-hand account was transcribed verbatim except for minor editing for clarity.

....

33 Lin, Sharat G. "Who Started It? Chronology of the Latest Crisis in the Middle East." *CounterPunch*, July 25, 2006. http://www.counterpunch.org/lin07252006. html

34 Ibid.

35 Ibid.

I was in Nabatiya, located near the Lebanese-Israeli border, with my husband, Adel, and our two small children when the Hezbollah-Israeli war broke out.

From the first days of the war we felt our lives were in danger. Helicopter gun ships hovered constantly overhead. Israeli planes raced across the sky, dropping their bombs God knows where. We knew it was just a matter of time before our village took a hit. My children, ages five and eight, were extremely nervous. My husband and I had great difficulty keeping them calm because, of course, we were stressed too.

Both of our families have homes in Nabatiya. This is where I bring the children each summer as soon as school ends. My husband joins me when he gets his vacation time. He works for a small company outside Madison, Wisconsin. Last summer I didn't get to Lebanon until the last week in June. The war, when it began, took us totally by surprise. And thankfully my husband had joined us by then. We didn't even know that the Hezbollah had kidnapped Israeli soldiers until after the fact. I used to be a news junkie when I lived here but I was on vacation and more interested in relaxing than keeping abreast of the news. I left that to the men and assumed that if anything of interest happened we would hear about it soon enough.

I have four siblings and each of us, along with our parents, has an apartment in the building my father built. My family and I are the only ones who moved away. Each evening we all congregated on my parents' terrace for a light dinner. It was their way of celebrating our return home for the summer.

I remember the night the war began. I arrived at my parents' with my children. My husband and the other men, including my father, were glued to the television. I could tell from the expression on their faces that something was seriously wrong. I went and stood behind my husband and heard the Israeli Prime Minister telling the Lebanese they were going to be bombed. "For what reason?" I blurted out before Adel told me about the kidnappings. "But those things have happened before. Remember when we saw an Israeli helicopter land nearby and kidnap some poor soul. And we've heard at least a few stories about Hezbollah slipping into northern Israel to kidnap some Israelis. So, why are things different now?"

I don't think an hour passed before we heard planes overhead. My children started crying. I tried to comfort them but it was a difficult thing to do when I was trembling myself. I don't remember if I ever went to the basement in our building but as soon as we heard the planes and understood what they had come to do, my siblings and I decided to check it out as a possible shelter.

On the one hand, the whole thing was like a nightmare scene while, at the same time, very surreal. I was on vacation and suddenly I was worrying about whether or not my family and I were going to die. Each of us rushed back to our respective apartment to get bedding, mattresses, water, flashlights, radio and anything else we might need. An hour later, we were all installed in what was to become our shelter for the next week. If there was a lull in the bombing we ventured out for groceries but I dared not let my children out of eyesight. This frustrated them enormously because while they were scared they did not realize the full extent of the danger.

I am not sure what a sixth sense is but one night I, we, all sensed intuitively that something was going to happen. One minute the bombing was particularly intense; the next minute there was an eerie silence. Questions started flying. Could the building sustain a hit? Who could know the answer to that? If the building wasn't safe, then where did we go? There came a moment, maybe it was that eerie silent moment, when we all knew that if we stayed put we were going to die. Flashlights in hand we ran up to the front entrance of the building. We talked aloud about where to go, in what direction. In the dark of night, we ran as fast as we could to a wooded area about a hundred meters from the house.

I actually think God himself pushed us out of the shelter because as soon as we reached the woods, a bomb fell on the building. We watched spellbound as one floor collapsed onto the next until there was nothing but a pile of rubble on the ground.

It was a strange and painful experience to watch part of my life disintegrating before my eyes. It was stranger still that those were my first thoughts when I should have been rejoicing that we were all alive and only homeless. On the other hand, I am thankful the realization of what happened crept up on me slowly instead of hitting me on the head like a bat. When it did I could not control my trembling or my tears as I hugged my

children to my chest, covering them with kisses and repeating over and over
again, "It's alright. We're going to be alright."

We spent the night in the woods not wanting to roam about in the
dark. The next day cousins, aunts and friends all wanted us to stay with
them. Two days later we heard that the Marines were evacuating Ameri-
cans. My husband and I decided to leave as quickly as we could. The bomb-
ing continued and my children needed to be rescued out of that inferno as
quickly as possible. I needed rescuing myself but mothers are supposed to
be brave and fearless.

Once we reached Cyprus and were able to get to the American Consul-
ate to arrange for travel documents we were airlifted back to the States. I
do not know what was worse, once we got back to Wisconsin: watching
the news and worrying about our family left behind or suffering the effects
of such a traumatic event. You are the first person I have talked to about
last summer's war. It has been too painful and frankly every time I think
about how lucky we were, how lucky I am to be alive and talking to you,
I burst into tears.[36]

. . .

While the Marines evacuated Americans, two thousand Israeli
troops, accompanied by tanks and armored bulldozers, moved
across the Lebanese border under the cover of a fierce barrage of
air strikes.

July 21 marked the first time that the United States responded
militarily to the conflict when the White House received a request
from Ehud Olmert and the Israeli Defense Forces (IDF) for pre-
cision-guided munitions. The request was quickly approved and
the munitions shipped via Scotland to Israel. US military experts
suggested this meant that Israel had expended most of its munitions in the first ten days. Apparently Israel was abandoning tacti-
cal bombing of Hezbollah assets and was poised for an onslaught
of what remained of Lebanon's infrastructure. During World

....

36   Author interview, Wisconsin, May 21, 2007.

War II the US and Britain destroyed Germany's sixty-six major population centers without any discernable impact either on German morale or military capabilities. Utilizing this same strategy did not seem logical.[37]

By the week of July 24 the fighting had intensified. The official cumulative death tolls reached 380 in Lebanon and thirty-seven in Israel. The World Health Organization estimated that up to six hundred thousand people, primarily in South Lebanon, had already been displaced.

. . .

On July 25 IAF missiles struck two clearly marked Red Cross ambulances traveling to Tyre with wounded civilians onboard. A day later Israeli missiles struck a refugee convoy waving white flags. These refugees were fleeing South Lebanon under Israeli orders. On July 28 Israeli Justice Minister Haim Ramon said that anyone who failed to obey the evacuation orders – which would have required dodging air strikes and circumnavigating bombed-out roads and bridges – would henceforth be considered fair game, effectively turning the south into a free-fire zone. "Anyone left in South Lebanon," he said, "is a terrorist."[38]

. . .

Karamallah Dagher lives in Marjayoun. He was a reporter for Reuters covering the war from South Lebanon.

When we were ordered to leave Marjayoun, the Lebanese Army made the arrangements. They called the UN command in South Lebanon to seek clearance from the Israelis to allow the refugees to be escorted out of Marjayoun. A few hours later, according to UN officials, the convoy received permission from Israel to leave.

....

37 Crooke, Alastair.

38 Wearing, David. "Britain's Role in the Israeli-Hezbollah War." *The Democrat's Diary*, September 7, 2006.

When two UN armored vehicles arrived in Marjayoun they found three thousand people, including Shiites from the surrounding devastated villages, waiting to leave. The 9:00 A.M. departure was delayed. Additional transportation had to be arranged. Unbeknownst to us at the time, the road ahead had been heavily bombed; it needed to be repaired before we could leave. It was 4:00 P.M. when the convoy finally crept out of Marjayoun. A Lebanese escort of 350 soldiers led the caravan; the UN vehicles followed up the rear. At Hasbaya, the northern limit of their operations, the UN vehicles were obliged to leave the caravan, dangerously exposing the refugees.

As the convoy approached the ancient Kifraya vineyards at Joub Jannine near the Bekaa Valley, disaster struck.

The first bomb hit the second car in the caravan. I got out of my car to survey the damage. A short distance away I saw my friend, Elie, standing there. He asked me if I had any spare gasoline. That's when the second missile struck and Elie's head and shoulders were blown away, right in front of my eyes. His daughter is sixteen. She jumped out of the car, screaming, "I want my Daddy, I want my Daddy," but he was gone. It was awful.

I rushed back to my car and attempted to carry my arthritic mother to safety but she complained that I was hurting her so I put her back in the passenger seat and sat beside her. I waited for a violent death which mercifully never came. It came instead to my friend, Collette, the wife of Marjayoun's mayor. She was beheaded in her Cherokee jeep. Six others also died in the attack; thirty-six were severely wounded.

It was sheer mayhem. We had clearance from the Israeli Army. I don't know what happened. The Israelis knew a civilian convoy was on the road. We had white flags on all the vehicles. Why did they fire missiles at us?[39]

. . .

On August 7 the IDF warned UN troops that they would be attacked if any attempt was made to repair any of the bombed out bridges in Lebanon. Three days earlier, in the Christian area of northern Bei-

39   Fisk, Robert. "The Truce that Won't Last." *Counterpunch*, August 14, 2006. http://www.counterpunch.org/fisk08142006.html

rut, Israel bombed bridges, thereby cutting what the UN described as the umbilical cord for humanitarian aid to Lebanon.

Frustrated by their inability to identify and destroy major Hezbollah military assets, the IAF began targeting schools, community centers and mosques, assuming, wrongly, that their inability to identify and interdict Hezbollah bunkers signaled Hezbollah's willingness to hide their major assets inside civilian centers.[40] In fact, Hezbollah had invested much effort into developing an elaborate system of tunnels and underground bunkers in the countryside and away from civilian centers.[41]

Israel also miscalculated Hezbollah's intelligence gathering capabilities. Over a period of two years Hezbollah intelligence officers had built a significant signals counterintelligence capability. Throughout the war their commanders were able to predict when and where Israeli fighters and bombers would strike. They had also identified key Israeli human-intelligence assets in Lebanon. In June 2006, just a month before the abduction of the two Israeli soldiers, Lebanese intelligence officials broke up an Israeli spy ring operating inside Lebanon, arresting sixteen people. Hezbollah intelligence officers were also able to feed back information to the Israelis on their militia's most important emplacements, with the result that the IAF identified key emplacements that did not exist.[42]

. . .

In early August, Human Rights Watch released a report detailing serious violations of the laws of war by the Israeli Defense Forces.[43] It found that in dozens of attacks Israeli forces struck an area with no apparent military target. In some cases, the timing

....

40 Crooke, Alastair.

41 Cook, Jonathan. "Revisiting the Summer War." *The Electronic Intifada*, August 16, 2007.

42 Ibid.

43 Wearing, David.

and intensity of the attack, the absence of a military target, as well as return strikes on rescuers, suggested that Israeli forces bombed indiscriminately.[44] In none of the cases documented by Human Rights Watch was there evidence to suggest that Hezbollah was in or near the area of bombing. Israel, according to HRW, repeatedly attacked both individual vehicles and entire convoys of civilians who heeded the Israeli warnings to abandon their villages, as well as humanitarian convoys and ambulances that were clearly marked.[45]

In an article in the *Irish Examiner*, Danny Grossman, Israeli director of the American Jewish Congress, disputed the HRW document. He claimed that a report, prepared by Reuven Erlich, a retired lieutenant colonel who heads the Intelligence and Terrorism Information Center and has close ties with the military leadership, including an office in the Israeli Defense Ministry, proves that Israeli attacks against Hezbollah targets in populated areas did not violate international law. According to his report, Hezbollah deliberately operated within civilian areas. It claimed that guerrillas stashed weapons in hundreds of private homes and mosques, fired rockets near UN monitoring posts and had fighters transporting missiles closely follow ambulances.[46]

HRW Director Ken Roth responded to this and similar charges in the March/April 2007 issue of *Tikkun*. "The summer of 2006 was a difficult summer for all of us in the human rights movement. I grew up with the Jewish tradition of critical probing, of factually and logically based discourse. Unfortunately, that is not the way many of our reports were responded to by certain leaders of the American Jewish community. They responded with deceptive arguments, making up facts, even name-calling. One challenge for

....

44 Ibid.

45 Ibid.

46 "Israel Provides Proof that Hezbollah Used Civilians as Human Shields."
    Irish Examiner, December 5, 2006. www.themiddleeastnow.com/news/
    proofhumanshields.html

all of us is how to improve the level of discourse. It does not serve any of us when the discourse stoops to the level that it did this past summer. It dishonors the Jewish tradition.

"I understand full well the fear for Israel's existence. However, I think many people are focused on the wrong threat. As terrible as suicide bombing is, as terrible as Katyusha rockets are, they are not threats to Israel's existence. The threat to Israel today is Iran and its apparent development of nuclear weapons. If I were running Israel I would be worried about preventing the emergence of a political movement in the Middle East that would make it feasible for someone like the current president of Iran to say, 'We can afford to lose a lot of Muslims in a nuclear exchange because there are many more of us than Jews in Israel.' We may never be able to preclude such an environment ... but part of an effective defense of Israel requires changing public morality around this question in the Middle East, making it intolerable to think that a nuclear weapon would ever be used against Israeli cities. This requires reaffirming, not ignoring, basic human rights laws."[47]

. . .

Toward the end of July 2006, US Secretary of State Condoleezza Rice began her visits to Beirut and Israel. She carried no specific proposals for a cease-fire or even a means of diffusing the crisis. Her main preoccupation appeared to be limited to finding a way to continue the war until Hezbollah was crushed.[48] According to Alastair Crooke, her inability or unwillingness to persuade President Bush to halt the fighting and her remark about the conflict as marking the birth pangs of a new Middle East destroyed her credibility in the Arab world.[49]

Meyrav Wurmser, an Israeli citizen whose husband, David,

....

47 Roth, Ken. "Reflections on Human Rights Work." *Tikkun*, Match/April 2007, p. 64.

48 Lin, Sharat G.

49 Crooke, Alastair.

was the senior Middle East advisor to Vice President Dick Cheney (he resigned in November 2007), says the Bush administration dragged its feet during Israel's assault on Lebanon because it was waiting for Israel to expand its attack on Syria.[50] "The neocons are responsible for the fact that Israel got a lot of time and space," says Wurmser. "They believed that Israel should be allowed to win. A great part of it was the thought that Israel should fight against the real enemy, the one backing Hezbollah. It was obvious that it was impossible to fight directly against Iran, but the thought was that Iran's strategic and important ally, Syria, should be hit."[51]

. . .

UN Resolution 1701, which halted the Israeli-Hezbollah war, was crafted by the US and its allies and presented to the Security Council on August 5, following negotiations between the US, Israel and France, which acted on behalf of the Lebanese. It called for Israel to cease its offensive actions but allowed necessary defensive operations to continue for another forty-eight hours. In the opinion of Robert Falk, professor emeritus of international law at Princeton University, "This was simply a final effort by the US to provide political cover for Israel to attempt to seize some vestige of military victory from the jaws of its defeat. Israel was not censured in any way for using the run-up to the ceasefire to further escalate its military presence in Lebanon, thereby suggesting that the UN is all too often a geopolitical tool for powerful superpowers rather than an instrument for the enforcement of international law."[52]

By contrast, Hezbollah was required to terminate all military actions entirely. On August 6 the Lebanese government rejected the resolution as a capitulation document. In what was seen as a

....

50 Cook, Jonathan. "Do America and Israel Want the Middle East Engulfed in Civil War?" *The Electronic Intifada*, December 19, 2006, p. 5.

51 Ibid.

52 Falk, Robert and Asli U. Bali. "International Law at the Vanishing Point." *Middle East Report* (MERIP), 241. http://www.merip.org/mer/mer241/falk_bali.html

clear attempt to position the Lebanese government as a rejectionist part, Secretary of State Rice commented that such reactions demonstrated "who is for peace and who isn't."[53] Since the document stated that the violence escalated as a result of Hezbollah's attack on Israeli soldiers on July 12, 2006, it implicitly named Hezbollah as the aggressor. No differentiation was made in the scale of violence and no party was named responsible for extensive damage to civilian infrastructure and hundreds of thousands of internally displaced persons.

Had the British notion of appropriate response, that of diplomacy to obtain the release of its sailors kidnapped by Iran been adopted, as opposed to Israel's military response in a similar situation, thousands of lives in Lebanon and Israel would have been spared. When diplomacy should have been the first option, why then did Ehud Olmert hastily declare war? According to Seymour Hersh and others, the war plans were already on the table and the Israelis were simply waiting for a valid pretext to execute them. Therefore, contrary to Tony Blair who opted for diplomacy over conflict because he did not want war with Iran, Olmert had a preordained plan. It was to crush Hezbollah and disarm them, thereby allowing the pro-American Lebanese government to regain full control of all of its territory, particularly South Lebanon. This theory begs, in turn, a more profound question. Was the Israeli government acting as an instrument of the Bush administration so that if the war plans succeeded Bush could declare victory? His need for some sort of victory in the Middle East was perhaps desperate.

One hundred fifty-eight Israelis lost their lives because Olmert chose to go to war. Thirty-nine were civilians; 119 were soldiers killed in combat. An additional four civilians died of heart attacks during the bombing. Sixteen thousand buildings in northern Israel sustained damage.

In Lebanon, 1,109 civilians died and 4,399 were wounded. Fif-

....

53   Ibid.

teen thousand homes were destroyed as were nine hundred businesses and factories, 630 roads, seventy-seven bridges, twenty-five
fuel stations and thirty-one utility plants. While there is no official
tally from Hezbollah, it was estimated by the number of funerals
held that 184 of their fighters died during the war.

In the end, Resolution 1701 does not provide a mechanism for
disarming Hezbollah. In the aftermath of the war, a number of
possible approaches were proposed, ranging from straight disarmament to the integration of Hezbollah forces into the national
defense structure as a sort of civil defense league or national
guard.

Given the number of crises that have erupted in Lebanon
since August 2006, not least of which is the bitter divide between
the Sunnis and Shiites, it is unlikely any reasonable solution will
emerge any time soon. Much depends on Iran, another outside
player in Lebanese affairs. If Iran is ascendant and defiant and continues to regard an armed Hezbollah as a necessary tool of its foreign policy, then the chances of integrating, decommissioning or
disarming Hezbollah remain very slim.[54] Much depends, too, on
the Bush administration's designs for a new Middle East which
could include the disintegration of Lebanon as we know it into
small, non-threatening, religion-based cantons, a model America
has already created in Iraq. Lebanon, after all, is but a collection
of dissident factions with seventeen different religious affiliations
haphazardly thrown together under colonial French rule. With no
geographic boundaries, the communities overlap each other in
every area of the country. If cantonized, Lebanon would revert to
tribal warfare, similar to the scenario in Iraq, with no chance of
survival as a nation. Is this then part of the birth pangs of a new
Middle East as envisioned by President Bush?

Israeli and American policy toward the Palestinians is also a
determining factor. The tragic situation in Gaza reflects a total

....

54   Salem, Paul. "The Future of Lebanon." *Foreign Affairs*, Volume 83, No. 6, pp.
     19–20.

US misunderstanding of the situation on the ground. Israel, too, is turning a blind eye to the possible infiltration of something far worse than Hamas, as evidenced by recent events in Lebanon. It is also opening the door to a possible civil war between the Palestinian factions. Neither scenario offers security for Israel.

5

ONE BATTLE,
TWO PERSPECTIVES

I was able to obtain these two interviews through contacts I have
in Lebanon and Israel. I agreed ahead of time not to reveal their
names and, in fact, I do not even know their real names. I also
agreed not to reveal the names of my sources for these interviews.
These interviews were taped via phone conversations and transcribed verbatim except, in the case of the Hezbollah fighter, for
minor editing to help with clarity.

A HEZBOLLAH FIGHTER

I am from Bint Jbeil, a village three miles north of the Israeli border.
According to my grandfather our hilltop village overlooking northern
Israel was established by the Phoenicians thousands of years ago when they
migrated from Jbeil (Byblos), north of what is today Beirut. Bint Jbeil, by
the way, means "Daughter of Byblos." And did you know that the word
"Bible" comes from Byblos?

Bint Jbeil is called the capital of Hezbollah. It is unfair, in my opin-
ion, to refer to it as a Hezbollah stronghold, as if this was a crime, without
fully understanding why and how all of South Lebanon, and Bint Jbeil in
particular, became a place of resistance. For eighteen years we lived under
Israeli occupation, that is to say, Israeli occupation of Lebanese land,
approximately fifteen percent of Lebanon.

I remember the exact moment I decided to join the resistance move-

ment. I was fifteen years old. The year was 1985. My father was herding his cows when Israeli troops entered Bint Jbeil, came into his field and shot him in the head without any provocation. He was not even carrying a gun. He was simply in his village on his own land in South Lebanon, tending his cows.

Because I was young and agile I was one of several young men assigned to observe Israeli troop movement. I did nothing else. Wherever they were I found a way to sneak up close enough to watch and mentally record everything they did. When they arose in the morning; what they ate for breakfast; where they carried out their patrols; how many soldiers participated and in which direction they traveled. I vividly remember one particular mission. It was a challenge because I had to carry it out alone. At the same time I felt privileged to be asked to undertake such a difficult task. It was crucial at this particular moment in time that we know everything the Israelis were doing and when and where they were doing it. I stood in a cold stream in Wadi Hanine, south of the village, hidden in brush, not moving, for three days. When it was safe to move so as to report what I had observed, I couldn't walk. My feet were frostbitten from the freezing water. So, I crawled back to the village to give my report. I was, of course, in terrible pain but I didn't care. I was willing to die if necessary to rid my village of Israeli soldiers. Though I would have done whatever was necessary, endured any hardship to end the occupation, in truth, my strength came from the brave people of Bint Jbeil. They were deeply committed to the survival of our village. I know this was not particular to Bint Jbeil but I can speak only of what I know personally. They abhorred injustice too. It was not something any of them practiced toward their neighbors and firmly believed that no one should act unjustly toward them. But more than anything they held a deep moral certainty of what was fair and right. This energy created a powerful force, one that eventually drove Israeli troops from Bint Jbeil and the whole of South Lebanon in May 2000.

Some residents in our village were forced to leave during the occupation. They were expelled because they would not work for the South Lebanon Army, Israel's proxy army. Others were at risk of being thrown into Khiam, the prison run by the same thugs. The energy and determination of those who remained in Bint Jbeil was surely the result of how we were *treated. The Israelis did what they could to destroy our humanity. They treated us like animals. As a result, the people rose up and resisted. Isn't this normal? After all, where there is occupation there will always be resistance.*

Many of our people were followers of Moussa el Sadr, a Shiite spiritual leader who created the Amal movement before mysteriously disappearing in Libya in the mid-'70s. This movement was formed to help the poor people of South Lebanon to get organized, to get health care, schools and other social services. It had nothing to do with a fight against Jewish or Christian people. They are, after all, also monotheistic religions and we all believe in the same God. So, our resistance to the Israelis was not because of religion but because of what they were doing to us. Let me tell you a little story. Before the '82 Israeli invasion there were still Jews living in Beirut. They had their own neighborhood near Bab Edriss. They were respected and no one paid attention to their religion. Beirut also has a synagogue which Israeli planes tried to destroy during the bombing in '82. There is also a Jewish cemetery in Beirut on Damascus Street near the Sodeco neighborhood. When that area was being rebuilt after the civil war ended in '90 some developers wanted the land where the cemetery is located. The Lebanese government said no out of respect for all bodies buried there, regardless of their religion.

The Palestinian leadership also shares some responsibility for what eventually happened to us. Of course, sooner or later Israel would have found a pretext to invade because they wanted control of the Litani River. Security on their northern border was just an excuse to invade but Arafat and his PLO gave them the excuse, repeatedly. As early as 1969, Palestinian guerrillas used our villages to carry out attacks into Israel. Naturally Israel retaliated. But when Israel invaded the first time in 1978, these same Palestinians fled north leaving us utterly at the mercy of the invading Israeli Army. Some stayed behind and became collaborators, working for the Israelis and the South Lebanon Army. The locals felt bitterly betrayed when this happened; so betrayed, in fact, that when the Israelis entered South Lebanon in 1982, the villagers were so happy to be rid of the Palestinian guerrillas who treated them badly that they greeted the Israeli soldiers with rose petals. Yes, that's right, rose petals!

Israel, because it was forced to leave Lebanon, and America, because it defends Israel no matter what it does, calls Hezbollah a terrorist organization because of our military operations. Most countries, including Israel and America, spend vast amounts of their financial resources in defense and weaponry and military operations. This is not particular to Hezbollah. America is run by a military industrial complex, and so is Israel for that matter, so how can they criticize us for defending our land against an illegal occupation?

The border with Israel heated up again in April 1996 when Israel bombed the UN camp in Qana killing over one hundred Lebanese civilians. Israel claimed it bombed the camp because Hezbollah fighters were inside. First of all, the UN soldiers would never have allowed us inside the camp because it is against all regulations. Secondly, I know for a fact that my Hezbollah brothers were at least 350 meters away from the UN camp and were firing on Israeli soldiers who were on the Lebanese side of their self-declared security zone laying land mines. In my book this made them fair targets.

After the Israeli withdrawal in 2000, the border area remained relatively calm. Hezbollah did repeatedly attack Israeli positions in the Shebaa Farms area but this is Lebanese soil and because of the continued Israeli occupation there aggression on our part was legitimate.

When the war began on July 12, Israel accused us of firing rockets into northern Israel. First of all, when Hezbollah kidnapped two Israeli soldiers on July 12, 2006 it was an action directed at soldiers, not civilians, and Hezbollah only began sending rockets into northern Israel after Israeli planes began targeting civilian areas in Lebanon. But I think everyone was surprised at how violently things turned on July 12, 2006.

I know I was momentarily taken aback. Yes, I anticipated at some point that Israel would find a pretext to attack us. We even knew about their military maneuvers. The unmanned drones we sent over Israel told us many things but it was nevertheless a surprise when Israel retaliated with such force. Our leader, Hassan Nasrallah, had planned to kidnap Israeli soldiers. In fact, he made no secret of his intentions.

Was it a case of bad judgment to kidnap the Israeli soldiers when we knew Israel was preparing its military forces? That is not for me to say. I serve Hassan Nasrallah. I am prepared to do whatever he asks of me, even if it means sacrificing my life. After all, we fight to defend and liberate our land. Is there a more powerful motive than that? After the war there was a lot of talk about Hezbollah's force. Military observers claim we are about two thousand fighters but aside from the small cell of men with whom I work and train I do not know my fellow Hezbollah brothers. I have a specific task, as do others in my small unit, but we work independently of others. I think this is our strength. We train over and over as a unit. Each unit has assigned tasks and we know how to execute them well. This is how we succeeded in defeating Israel.

I will never forget the battle for Bint Jbeil. To begin with, I do not understand how Israel could have so underestimated the degree to which people would fight to save their land. Is it because in previous wars Israel fought not on their own land but on Arab land for territorial expansion?

When Israeli troops entered Bint Jbeil on July 26th, they probably assumed they were entering a deserted village because there was no visible sign of life. I later learned that their commanders back in Israel were telling the press that the village would be theirs in a matter of hours. We watched the soldiers enter the village. We knew ahead of time from which direction they would be crossing. Of the possible twenty-four entry points we had narrowed it down to just three. As I said before, one of our greatest strengths is that we know everything about them and they seemingly know so little about us. At any rate, when they came into the empty marketplace we ambushed them from three sides, firing RPGs (rocket propelled grenades), anti-tank missiles and mortar rounds. The soldiers quickly took cover inside one of the buildings, effectively trapping themselves inside. A fierce battle erupted but the soldiers had no where to go. When several Merkava tanks and transport vehicles came to their rescue, we fired on them too, setting them on fire. I was told that some eight or nine soldiers died in just that attack alone. A short time later Bint Jbeil came under heavy bombardment. The Israeli Air Force bombed for eleven straight hours, took a break and continued again the next day for a straight twenty-one hours, until large swaths of our village were destroyed. Bombs were even dropped on a flock of sheep in a field adjacent to Bint Jbeil. After the battle the animals' owner half joked that his sheep were surely the most *valuable in all of Lebanon because Israel probably spent a couple million dollars in bombs to kill them.*

I was in no position to tell you how many residents were left in Bint Jbeil when the battle began but I can tell you that before it ended many residents suddenly appeared with their machine guns and rifles – in the alleyways, behind barricades and anyplace they could take aim – and began firing on the soldiers. The Israeli government claimed we used civilians as shields, a claim they always make by the way, but not in Bint Jbeil. No one forced these people out into the streets. They came out on their own. They were mad at losing their homes, their businesses, their schools, their mosques. They fought to defend their village and were prepared to die if necessary.

Many Israeli soldiers were killed in the five-day battle in Bint Jbeil. That must have been a great shock to the mighty Israeli military establishment. But if the rumors that the Israelis planned to use llamas to deliver supplies to their soldiers inside Lebanon are true, and that the plan was abandoned because the animals simply sat down instead of walking into the battle zone, then I have to wonder why the mighty Israeli Army was not as smart as the llamas! It was the famous Golani Infantry Brigade, by the way, that walked into our trap.

Bint Jbeil, for the Israelis, was symbolic. When Israeli troops withdrew in May 2000, our leader, Hassan Nasrallah, celebrated this historic event by holding a parade here. This did not sit well with the Israelis and they hoped this time around to score a major victory. We deprived them of that!

A year after the war, and despite the fact that Bint Jbeil was practically reduced to rubble, we have been most fortunate compared to many villages still in total disrepair. We have the government of Qatar to thank for helping us rebuild our village. They arrived with cash as soon as the war ended. Yes, they are a predominantly Sunni country but they disregarded the so-called Sunni-Shiite divide and decided to extend a helping hand to their fellow Arab brothers. Hezbollah also helped, providing much needed relief supplies. Many buildings have been repaired, if not totally rebuilt. Shops are open for business and our children are back in makeshift schools.

Neshkor Allah! *(Thanks be to God.)*

AN ISRAELI SOLDIER

I am a member of the Golani Brigade of the Israeli Defense Forces. I'm lucky to be alive and I'm very grateful to my buddies for having carried me out of the inferno, gotten me onto a helicopter and back to Haifa for treatment.

On July 26, 2006, our unit was ordered into South Lebanon. I'm not supposed to talk about my feelings because an IDF soldier is tough and always battle ready. But this time when I crossed the border my heart sank to my stomach. I lost my best friend to one of Hezbollah's roadside bombs in 2000 shortly before we withdrew and the last thing I ever wanted to do was return to this rugged, rocky death trap of a country, where Hezbollah fighters know every shrub and rock formation and could be hiding anywhere. And if rumors were correct, they now had some of the most sophisticated weaponry in the world. Alright, I'll say it: I felt like I was walking to my death!

There were other unsettling things too about this war which added to my anxiety. Rumors abounded about reserve units being sent to the front without proper training. These were the guys who were supposed to back us up. They had outdated equipment and no body armor. This sounds like a description of a third world ragtag army, not the IDF! My cousin who is a reservist told me he was sent into South Lebanon without the munitions to carry on the fight. No one in his unit had a bulletproof vest. Water and rations took twenty-four hours to reach his unit. What kind of a battle plan was this? Were we all just sacrificial lambs so Olmert and Peretz could show the world how tough they were, how ready and willing they were to destroy Hezbollah for George Bush?

And there's another thing that didn't bode well with a lot of us. Our Air Force had already spent almost two weeks carpet bombing the South without much success. What the hell were we supposed to be able to accomplish?

So there I was marching toward Bint Jbeil, a small village less than three miles from the Israeli border. From a distance it looks like a lovely village surrounded by wildflowers even in the heat of the summer. In some other life I might have been walking to a neighbor's garden party. Our military commanders hate Bint Jbeil because it was here that Hezbollah celebrated with great fanfare our hasty retreat in May 2000. What was then-Prime Minister Ehud Barak ever thinking when he suddenly withdrew our troops as though they were thieves in the dead of night?

We were some minutes behind an advance patrol up ahead. Just before we got to the outskirts of Bint Jbeil, we heard shots and explosions. It was obvious our soldiers up ahead were taking hits but there was nothing we could do. We were pinned down and in fact I ran inside a building and up to the second floor to try to locate the source of fire. Hezbollah had eyes everywhere. They were watching our every move and like idiots we walked right into their trap. I didn't even have time to sneak a look outside a window when a missile hit the house. In the momentary stillness after the explosion, I could hear our radio operator on the ground floor calling in our location and asking for help. I was relieved but before I could cross the room to the stairs a second missile exploded within feet of where I was standing. The blast knocked me up against the wall. My chest and arms got sprayed with shrapnel. I was momentarily blinded by a bright light before the room filled with smoke. I had difficulty breathing. I wanted to cough but when I tried I felt excruciating pain across my chest. And when I saw the gaping holes in my arms I almost passed out. I learned later that the metal shards had broken multiple bones in each arm. The medic in our unit tended to my wounds as best he could and taped up my arms. In the meantime we learned that a helicopter couldn't get close enough to evacuate us, because of the fighting, so we had to find a way to get closer to the border. I'm not sure how my buddies managed. All I remember is leaning on two strong shoulders and was told repeatedly to keep my feet moving until we got to a point where we could safely board the helicopter back to Haifa.

From my hospital bed I learned that we lost nine soldiers that day. Another twenty-two were badly wounded. Within another twenty-four hours, without a single success on the battleground, Olmert called up three more reserve divisions, a full fifteen thousand troops. On July 28 an intelligence leak published in Israeli newspapers claimed that Hezbollah had yet to suffer any significant loss of military capabilities. Olmert and Peretz denied this and ordered the war to continue. Reserve soldiers make up seventy percent of the Israeli Army and unlike the enlisted men they are free to speak out. And speak out they have since the war, protesting the way they were forced, unprepared and poorly equipped, into battle.

All these months later do I regret having gone into Lebanon? Of course not! I love my country and we needed to fight this war to secure our northern border. Any doubts I have about this conflict deal more with preparedness and where we are as a nation now that the war has ended. Are we more secure now than we were before the war? Did we achieve our goal of destroying Hezbollah? Our kidnapped soldiers have not been returned and 119 of our soldiers died in battle. Yes, we now have UNIFIL and NATO troops on our border as a buffer but Hezbollah is still armed and dangerous and well-entrenched across the rocky terrain of South Lebanon. This is an important point and one I find very troubling. I am young and don't want to spend my whole life preparing for war. In Israel we have a war mentality. We never seem to talk about peace. It is as if saying that word is being disloyal to the State. I'm ready to live in peace with my neighbors. I think Hezbollah would do the same. Why aren't our leaders willing to take the leap?

As I said earlier, I am no stranger to Lebanon but this time around Hezbollah was using a broad range of anti-tank missiles including American-made TOWs. Back in the '80s, when I last encountered them, they were a militia. Now, they are a full fledged army trained and equipped by Syria and Iran, at least that's what I am told. But then, we're equipped by the US so what's the difference. In this war it wasn't army versus army warfare. It was army versus guerrilla warfare tactics. They drew us in like bees to honey and then pounded us almost to death.

In the end, this is their territory they are defending. We would surely do the very same thing if someone came into our country and tried to take our land.

CLUSTER BOMBS AND OTHER ENVIRONMENTAL HAZARDS

In the aftermath of the 2006 war, the people of South Lebanon had to contend with hundreds of thousands of cluster bombs dropped by Israel in the last seventy-two hours of the conflict, after a UN ceasefire had been reached but before it came into effect.

Unlike landmines, which are designed to maim as much as kill, cluster bombs contain more explosive power and metal fragmentation, making them more likely to kill and to cause multiple casualties. When cluster bombs strike they set off pressure waves within the body which do horrific damage to soft tissue and organs. Even a single fragment can rupture the spleen or cause the intestines to explode. Victims who survive may suffer from loss of limbs, burns, puncture wounds, ruptured eardrums and blindness.[55]

A cluster bomb consists of a canister designed to open in mid-air and disperse smaller submunitions referred to as bomblets. The bomblets – a single canister can hold hundreds, ranging in size from a soda can to a flashlight battery – are packed with shrapnel and an explosive charge. Cluster bombs are area weapons. This means they are not designed to attack a precise target but rather to

....

55 "Two People an Hour Killed or Injured by Cluster Munitions." *Handicap International*, September 24, 2007. www. handicap-international.org.uk/page_247. pfp

destroy all potential targets in a given area. Depending on the type of munitions and the delivery system, the footprint of one cluster bomb can be as large as one square kilometer or about two hundred fifty acres. Cluster bombs were originally designed to attack enemy forces lined up on a battlefield, to impede or slow advancing troops or destroy or render airfields unusable. According to Scott Stedjan, the National Coordinator of the United States Campaign to Ban Landmines, the US Army Infantry Division, in 2003, labeled cluster munitions as "losers" and suggested they were "a Cold War relic" and were not for use in urban areas.[56]

Contrary to the terms of the US Arms Export Control Act that forbids the use of such weapons in populated areas, the Bush administration, at the height of the July 2006 war, rushed through a request from Israel for more than one thousand three hundred American-made M26 cluster bombs. The first major shipment of American-made cluster bombs to Israel was ordered by President Nixon during the Yom Kippur War in October 1973 when then-Israeli Prime Minister Golda Meir threatened to use nuclear weapons to stop Israel from being overrun by Arab forces.[57]

The Mutual Defense Assistance Agreement, which was in effect when the United States provided Israel its cluster bombs in 1973, stipulated that Israel "will not undertake any act of aggression against any other state."[58]

In 1982, when Israel dropped cluster bombs over Lebanon, President Ronald Reagan immediately suspended any additional shipments of cluster bombs to Israel. Currently, Human Rights Watch estimates that the US has a stockpile of one billion old, unreliable and inaccurate cluster munitions and the Defense

....

56 Stedjan, Scott and Laura Weis. "The Cluster Bomb Treaty." *CounterPunch*, March 20, 2007.

57 Lamb, Franklin. "Israel's Gifts to Lebanon." Excerpt from *A Quarter Century of Israel's Use of American Weapons in Lebanon (1978–2006)*. Accessed September 24, 2007. www.ifamericansknew.org/cur_sit.html

58 Tzinis, Irene A. Recorded by Titus Peachey. "Then and Now: Israel, Lebanon and Cluster Bombs." http://mcc.org/clusterbombs/news/lebanon/thenandnow.html

Department continues, despite the ban imposed by President Reagan, to transfer them to allies around the world.[59]

In the closing days of the 2006 war, the Israeli military fired thousands of cluster munitions into South Lebanon. International demining groups estimate that these weapons contain some 2.6 million to four million bomblets, around ninety percent of which were fired during the last seventy-two hours of the conflict. As of February 14, 2007, the UN Mine Action Coordination Center (UNMACC) in South Lebanon had identified 847 cluster bomb strike locations, contaminating a total of thirty-four million square meters of land. Since the UN-brokered ceasefire went into effect on August 14, 2006, UNMACC has reported 216 civilian and demining casualties in South Lebanon, thirty deaths and 186 serious injuries.[60]

· · ·

Salima Barakt has been a widow for the last eighteen years. She lives with her two children, Maryam, forty-two, and Ali, twenty-three, in Yohmour, a small village in South Lebanon. Maryam is blind and mentally disabled. Ali is also mentally disabled. As the sole breadwinner, Salima works in the fields growing tobacco and caring for the olive trees in her orchard.

I have lived through all the wars in South Lebanon but this war was the worst. I decided to stay in my home because it was too hard to flee with my two children. However, the bombs disturbed them. They began yelling and screaming and in desperation I fled to my parents' house in another part of my village. As soon as the ceasefire took effect, we returned to our house. There were cluster bombs everywhere. I remember my father carefully pushing a cluster bomb off the road with his foot so my children wouldn't step on it.

There was a tremendous amount of debris on the steps going down to

········

59 Berrigan, Frida. "From Kosovo to Lebanon, Cluster Bomb Casualties Continue to Mount." *In These Times*, December 2006.

60 Stedjan, Scott and Laura Weis.

*my house so I got a broom to sweep it out of the way. There was a terri-
ble explosion and I woke up in the hospital. I suffered severe injuries to
my head, my stomach, and my legs. I willed myself to live because of my
children.*

*I want to ask the Israelis why they did this to me. I am an innocent
woman. I am not involved in politics. Please tell Condoleezza Rice to stop
sending these bombs to Israel. I wish she would get married and have children so that she will know what it feels like to see your children suffering
from the bombs. Tell Miss Rice that we have had enough. We cannot take
it anymore.*

Though the war is over, Salima's life has forever changed. She
knows there are still bombs in her orchards. The medicines needed
to treat her children are expensive yet she is no longer able to work
because of the injuries she sustained.[61]

. . .

Of the 1,109 Lebanese civilians killed in the thirty-four-day war,
one-third were children. Unexploded cluster bombs continue to
take a toll, particularly among the youth.

Raed Moukalled is an optician in Nabatieh. One day in December 1999, he took his two sons to play in the park. This is an area of
the city where families go to relax and have picnics so Raed had no
reason to think that there would be any danger.

*My boys ran off to play. Suddenly there was a dreadful explosion. My
five year old son, Ahmad, had picked up a strange object that looked like
a colored bottle. The cluster bomb exploded in his hands. Two days later,
he died.*

Raed's life has dramatically changed since the accident. He
pours his energy into making sure that other parents are aware of
the dangers of cluster bombs by participating in community aware-
ness campaigns.

We have to make the connection between the laws and policies of gov-

....

61 "Salima." Recorded by Titus Peachey. http://www.mcc.org/clusterbombs/news/
lebanon/reports/salima.html

*ernments and people. I am a human being. I am not a terrorist. We have
laws to protect the panda ... but what about laws to protect our children?*

The bomb that killed Ahmad on December 2, 1999 was
dropped over South Lebanon by Israel during its 1982 invasion,
which means this bomb lay in wait for seventeen years. Ahmad, the
boy who died, was not even alive when that bomb was dropped.[62]

. . .

While designed to detonate on impact, cluster bomblets typically
fail to detonate as intended approximately five to thirty percent
of the time, leaving behind large numbers of hazardous explosive
duds that are akin to landmines, injuring and killing civilians and
contaminating the land long after the conflicts end. The UNMACC
in South Lebanon estimates that as many as forty percent of Israeli
cluster bombs used during the conflict failed to explode, leaving as
many as 1,126,400 unexploded bomblets in the southern part of
the country. They can lie for years, often difficult to see because of
their small size, on roofs, in gardens, in trees, alongside the roads,
even in rubbish, waiting to explode when touched. If Lebanon's
future mirrors that of other countries affected by cluster bombs,
civilians will be impacted by these weapons for years to come. Cluster bombs dropped on Laos in 1973 are still injuring people in that
country. In the past thirty years, twelve thousand Laotian civilians,
many of whom were not born when the bombs were dropped, have
died from contact with an unexploded cluster dud.[63]

Thankfully, the international community has begun to take
action. In February 2007, Norway hosted the Oslo Conference
on Cluster Munitions. Forty-nine countries met to discuss how to
address the indiscriminate and lasting effects of cluster munitions
on civilians. At the conference forty-six countries agreed to a land-
mark decision that by 2008 they would sign a legally binding treaty

---

62 "Raed." Recorded by Titus Peachey. http://www.mcc.org/clusterbombs/news/
lebanon/reports/raed.html

63 Stedjan, Scott and Laura Weis.

prohibiting the use, production, transfer, and stockpiling of cluster munitions. Half of the world's thirty-four producer countries, one-third of the world's stockpiling countries, six users or former users, and six affected states signed the Oslo declaration. The Bush administration did not send a delegation to the Oslo meeting.[64]

. . .

Why did Israel use cluster bombs in the last hours of the war? Military analysts on the ground in South Lebanon suggest two possible reasons: to inflict collective punishment on the Lebanese for their support of Hezbollah; and a desire by Israel to get rid of as much of its US cluster bomb inventory as possible. The Pentagon had stipulated that Israel's inventory had to be reduced to a lower level before Israel could reorder newer models. This is probably why the thirty-three-year-old model, shipped in '73 by President Nixon, was used so widely across the south. Israel was simply cleaning out its cluster bomb unit closet.[65]

According to a commander in the IDF's Multiple Launch Rocket System (MLRS) unit in an article published in *Haaretz* on September 19, 2006, the IDF fired some eighteen hundred cluster rockets on Lebanon during the war and they contained over 1.2 million cluster bombs. He also confirmed that the IDF used cluster shells fired by 155 mm. artillery cannons, so the number of cluster bombs fired on Lebanon was even higher. "In Lebanon," he testified, "we covered entire villages with cluster bombs. What we did there was crazy and monstrous." These targets were described, according to him, as "General Staff targets."[66] This description was given to targets authorized by the Chief of Staff's office. It was also the same office that authorized the type of specific munitions used during the thirty-four-day war.

....

64 Ibid.

65 Lamb, Franklin. "Israel's Use of American Cluster Bombs." *CounterPunch*, September 14, 2006.

66 Hasson, Nir and Meron Rapoport. "IDF Admits Targeting Civilian Areas in Lebanon with Cluster Bombs." *Haaretz*, November 21, 2006.

The IDF used MLRS rockets, according to the commander, even though they are known to be very inaccurate. The rockets' deviation from the target reaches to around one thousand two hundred meters. A substantial percentage of these rockets do not explode and become mines. In order to compensate for the rockets imprecision, the order was to "flood" the area with them. "We had no option of striking an isolated target and the commanders knew this very well," he said. In at least one instance they were asked to fire cluster rockets toward "village outskirts" in the early morning. "They told us that this is a good time because people are coming out of the mosques and the rockets would deter them."

In other cases, they fired the rockets at a range of less than fifteen kilometers, even though the manufacturer's guidelines state that firing at this range considerably increases the number of duds.[67]

Soldiers in the artillery corps testified that the IDF also ordered the use of phosphorous shells which, according to many experts, is prohibited by international law.

A direct hit from a phosphorous shell causes severe burns and a painful death. In 2006 there was an international scandal after a television crew presented horrific photos of the charred bodies of Iraqis injured by phosphorous bombs during the course of the American attack on the city of Fallujah. I know, too, that Israel used phosphorous bombs during its carpet bombing over Beirut in the summer of '82. Doctors at hospitals reported bodies of young children smoldering for hours after being pronounced dead. The American *Book of War*, published in 1999, which sets down the rules of war for the American Army, states: "The ground war law prohibits the use of phosphorous against human targets." The pact on prohibiting or limiting flammable weapons bans the use of phosphorous against civilian targets and against military tar-

. . . .

67 Rapoport, Meron. "When Rockets and Phosphorous Cluster." *Haaretz*, September 13, 2006.

gets found amid large civilian populations.[68] According to the IDF spokesperson, "International law does not contain a sweeping ban on the use of cluster bombs. The Conventional Weapons Pact does not stipulate a ban on the use of inflammatory weapons, i.e. phosphorous, either. Rather, it only offers rules for organizing the use of this weapon."[69]

Article 51 of the UN Charter acknowledges the right of all states to individual or collective self-defense and to raise armies and procure armaments to that end. However, Article 51 is not absolute. International humanitarian law calls for a balance to be struck between the military utility of a particular weapon and its humanitarian consequences.[70]

Hezbollah also fired cluster bombs, though on a much smaller scale. Human Rights Watch documented two Chinese-made rockets that contained thirty-nine pellet-filled bomblets each. Israeli police say Hezbollah fired 113 cluster rockets among the nearly four thousand Katyushas that rained down on northern Israel.

Hezbollah rockets caused numerous forest fires inside northern Israel, particularly near Kiryat Shmona. As many as sixteen thousand five hundred acres of land, including forests and grazing fields, were destroyed. The Jerusalem National Fund estimates that it will take fifty to sixty years to rehabilitate the forests.[71]

. . .

After the cease-fire on August 14, many people anxiously returned to their villages only to find their homes destroyed and the area around them too dangerous to walk. The United Nations estimates that thirty percent of South Lebanon's cultivatable land was affected by cluster bombs. Crops like olives, grapes, citrus fruits and tobacco make up seventy percent of South Lebanon's economy. An estimated ninety percent of the local population depends

....

68   Ibid.
69   Ibid.
70   Stedjan, Scott and Laura Weis.
71   *Jerusalem National Fund Report*, August 9, 2006.

on agriculture. For the farmers whose lands are affected, this spells disaster. Despite the dangers, those who insist on returning to their fields will find the work tedious, picking through green weeds and rocky terrain for tennis ball-sized bomblets that can explode with the slightest touch. One bomblet that was recently found had buried itself on impact a foot underground.

Every few feet in the hillside village of Yohmor, near the Litani River and five kilometers from the Israeli border, you can find some kind of unexploded ammunition or a cluster bomb – on the roofs of houses, in the gardens, scattered across fields, along the sides of roads. They are even inside houses. I know of one instance where a bomblet landed in a pile of logs beside the fireplace. Unfortunately the small child playing nearby spotted it. Because it looked like one of his toys he grabbed it. He lost both of his arms in the explosion.

The British-based Mines Advisory Group (MAG) has been working with the UN Mine Action Coordination Center in villages like Yohmor. When the initial work begins, MAG divides its teams' work into three phases. First, they clear roads and paths and inside houses. Phase two is clearing about five meters around the house. Phase three clears the entire village. In one house alone a MAG team found thirty-two explosives.

. . .

Nayef, a deminer working in South Lebanon, explained his job to me.

I am a medic by profession and I volunteer with the Red Cross whenever there is a crisis, like the summer war with Israel. I have also been trained as a deminer and that is what I am currently doing full-time.

When a team of deminers enters a village for the first time, they try to meet with the mayor. He gives them the demographics – number of people who normally live there, location of buildings, roads and anything else that might make their job a little easier. The mayor has usually had time to survey the damage too and can give the deminers an indication of the approximate location of the bombs. Then the team gets to work. By the way, our team always includes a medic and his ambulance. They keep their distance from our work area, approximately 150 meters, in case there is an accident, but they are there to assist if ever we need emergency care.

If a field is covered with bomblets, the deminers cordon it off with barbed wire, then hang huge red banners and signs around it advising people to stay away. If the contaminated area is a house, they do the same but cordon off the entire perimeter around the house as well. One person on our team enters the field first to determine what kinds of bombs are on the ground and how dangerous they are. If it is a large bomb and too fragile to move, it is detonated right where it lies, obviously with all precautions taken to protect us and anyone in the vicinity. Once that is done, we don our protective jacket and helmet, turn on our detector machine and enter the field, walking one baby step at a time. We work in teams of three but if the area is large we might be five, sometimes more.

The moment I step onto that field I am only concentrated on where my foot goes and what the detector is telling me. Nothing else matters. I guess I should say nothing else should matter but it is very hot here in the summer. On the job I am wearing a helmet with thick face covering and a heavy protective jacket, both of which make me sweat a lot. The perspiration that pours off my forehead and into my eyes is salty and makes my eyes string. This is the kind of distraction I sometimes have and of course if I do something careless, even move the wrong way, it could cost me my life so every second on the job is stressful.

The hardest part of my job is the psychological stress. It goes without saying that a deminer must be physically fit but he must also be mentally sound. I know myself that no matter what may have happened earlier in the morning, when I get to my job and I enter a room that I assume is full of bomblets I cannot afford to think of anything else except finding those bombs. Even if my child is quite ill or I have had a fight with my neighbor, I cannot bring those stresses to my job.

I remember one day when I thought I would lose it. My team and I were called urgently to come to a village. A woman had returned to her home. I don't know what she could have been thinking. She surely must have known her village was covered with cluster bombs yet she walked inside her house and began picking up things that had fallen on the floor. She *must have suddenly realized that she was in a room full of bombs because she panicked and started screaming over and over, "There are bombs here. I'm going to die." Fortunately for her someone heard her and called us. By the time I reached her front door she was in a state of sheer hysteria. I could not calm her down and wasn't even sure how I was going to get her out of the house safely since she was uncontrollable. I didn't know what to do so I slapped her face. Not hard but just enough to bring her to her senses. I am not sure who was more startled, the lady or me, but it worked and I was able to lead her outside to safety. Of course she had every reason to be hysterical. Her whole floor was covered with bomblets. My team and I spent most of the day clearing them out.*

So while I try not to focus on dying or whether or not I will see my family again, and only think about finding the bombs, my days are enormously stressful. The demining company I work for thinks it will take upwards of seven to ten years of hard work to rid South Lebanon of all the bomblets left by the war. I pray I will stay alive and well, both physically and mentally, so I can continue this important work. Inchallah!

. . .

Human Rights Watch has asked Israel to provide information to the UN Mine Action Coordination Center on the location of its cluster munitions attacks and the specific weapons used. They ask that Israel also provide technical, financial and material assistance to facilitate the marking and clearance of cluster duds and other explosive remnants of war. American Task Force for Lebanon, a Washington-based NGO headed by Dr. George Cody, has also asked Secretary of State Rice to pressure Israel to comply.

To date, Israel has not responded to either of these requests.

. . .

The Lebanese government estimates that more people will die from the long-term effects of pollution caused by Israel's bombing than were killed in the actual war. The environmental damage began when Israel bombed a fuel storage tank at the Jiyyeh power station eighteen miles south of Beirut on July 13. The government managed to repair the damage and prevent an oil spill. However, two days later, Israeli bombs struck again, hitting the same tank which is located just twenty-five meters from the sea. The strike fatally damaged the tank's protective berm, a concrete and earth barrier designed to stop any oil spilling from the tank to reach the sea, spewing four million gallons of oil. This is the largest oil spill to date in the eastern Mediterranean.

The bombing also caused a massive fire which produced a highly poisonous cloud that hung over a third of the country for twelve days. Tests have since shown that the cloud contained high levels of poisonous lead, mercury and highly dangerous polychlorinated biphenyls (PCB).

"Not only have we been breathing this for days but all the agricultural produce has been subjected to this pollution," said Yacoub Sarraf, Lebanon's Environmental Minister. "Even worse, all these poisons will come down with the rain and will seep through the soil and into our water table."

A year after the Jiyyeh bombing, the sea along the Lebanese coastline is still spitting out black poison despite efforts to clean up the mess. Greenpeace described the spill, which polluted about 150 kilometers of the Lebanese coast, as an underwater nightmare and a time bomb because oil sunk to the seabed. The environmental group estimates it will take at least another year to clean up the spill. One of the major obstacles hampering the clean-up is the political crisis gripping the country which triggered the resignation of the Environmental Minister.

A UN team tested the soil over a five square kilometer area around the plant and detected elevated levels of polycyclic aromatic hydrocarbons (PAH) – petroleum products linked to a wide range of health risks. They recommended that people living close to the plant be subjected to long-term monitoring in order to pick up any unusual health trends such as cancers and heart problems.

According to a UN report issued on January 23, 2007, many of the bombed and burnt out factories and industrial complexes, including the Jiyyeh power plant, remain contaminated with a variety of toxic and health hazardous substances such as ashes, oils, heavy metals, industrial chemicals, rubble, solid waste and sewage. All represent a threat to water supplies and public health. Dealing with and disposing of significant quantities of war-related debris, including health care and hospital waste, continues to represent a major environmental challenge. The sheer volume of the debris is overwhelming. Lebanon's water supply and sewage networks also suffered extensive damage and continue to present a risk of groundwater contamination and a potential public health hazard.

. . .

It is worth repeating here that UN Resolution 1701, which halted the war, was crafted by the United States and its ally, Israel. Since the document states that the violence escalated as a result of Hezbollah's attack on Israeli soldiers on July 12, 2006, it implicitly names Hezbollah as the aggressor. No differentiation was made in the scale of violence and no party was named responsible for extensive damage to civilian infrastructure that amounted to close to $5 billion.

To the charge that Israel deliberately bombed the Jiyyeh facility, a spokesman for the government replied: "We deny Lebanon's accusations. They seem to be ridiculous. We never deliberately targeted any civilian capacity or place. We only targeted places or facilities relevant to Hezbollah."

According to UN Secretary-General Ban Ki-Moon, since August 14, 2006, 180 civilians have been injured and twenty-three have died as a result of cluster munitions. "I regret to have to report that, despite a number of attempts by UN senior officials to obtain information regarding the firing data of cluster munitions utilized during last summer's conflict, Israel has yet to provide this critical data. I call on the Government of Israel once again to provide this information to the United Nations."

. . .

If large swaths of Israel had been pounded to dust by an aggressive Arab neighbor, if its coastline and industrial zones had sustained devastating levels of environmental damage and pollution, the world would have reacted with anger and indignation, and rightly so. Where is the outrage when such deeds are perpetrated by Israel? Why is there a double standard with Israel particularly, as in this instance when it deserves condemnation for its wanton destruction of South Lebanon? It is a member of the world body of nations. As such, it should be held to the same standards as everyone else.

If not, and if its perceived indifference to Arab life also continues, Israel runs the risk of convincing many in the region that long-term coexistence with Israel is impossible.

7
WATER WARS
AND LAND GRABS:
THE LITANI RIVER
AND THE SHEBAA FARMS

LITANI RIVER

It was in 1937, in an address to the Zionist World Worker's Party in Zurich, that David Ben-Gurion, then chairman of the Jewish Agency, first unveiled his intention to destabilize and dismember Lebanon in order to install a puppet regime pliable to Israeli demands and take its water.

"Lebanon is a natural ally of the Jews of the land of Israel," said Ben-Gurion. "The proximity of Lebanon will furnish a loyal ally for the Jewish State as soon as it is created and will give us the possibility to expand to the Litani River, with the agreement and benediction of our neighbors who need us."[72]

Ben-Gurion, as it turns out, was not the first to formulate a strategy for Lebanon and its water. On November 5, 1918, a committee of British mandate officials and Zionist leaders put forth a suggested northern boundary for a Jewish Palestine "from the North Litani River in Lebanon up to the Banias River in Syria."

....

72 Randall, Jonathan C. *Going All the Way: Christian Warlords, Israeli Adventurers and the War in Lebanon.* Vintage Books, New York, 1984, pp. 188–189.

In 1919, at the Paris Peace Conference, Zionist leaders proposed boundaries that would have incorporated the Lebanese district of Bint Jbeil and all the territories up to and including the Litani River. The proposal emphasized the vital importance of controlling all water resources.[73]

At the same conference both David Ben-Gurion and Chaim Weizmann, who would become Israel's first Prime Minister and first president respectively, tried to persuade the Maronite Patriarch Hayek, who headed the Lebanese delegation, to abandon South Lebanon in return for a promise of technical and financial assistance to develop the area to the north, the area Israel hoped would become a Christian state.[74]

Instead, the Maronites chose the alternative of peace with the Muslims, establishing the 1943 National Pact which succeeded in preserving Christian dominance and prosperity for three decades.[75]

Determined to succeed one way or another, Israeli forces managed to reach the Litani River in 1949 and occupy part of the district of Marjayoun and Bint Jbeil. International pressure, however, forced Israel to withdraw. In 1954, the Israeli government tried again to renew its claim on the Litani. President Eisenhower attempted to diffuse the crisis by sending his envoy, Eric Johnston, who proposed a formula of sharing the Litani among Lebanon, Syria and Israel. Israel rejected the proposal and threatened to use force against the Lebanese government to prevent its utilization of the Litani to develop South Lebanon.[76]

The political designs of David Ben-Gurion and his penchant for the use of force over diplomacy to destabilize Lebanon and

....

73 Chomsky, Noam. Preface to *Israel's Sacred Terrorism: A Study Based on Moshe Sharett's Personal Diary*, 3rd Edition. Livia Rokach. AAUG Press, Belmont, MA, 1980, p. 3.

74 Ibid.

75 Chomsky, Noam. *The Fateful Triangle: The United States, Israel and the Palestinians*. South End Press, Boston, 1983, p. 183.

76 Chomsky, Noam. Preface to *Israel's Sacred Terrorism*.

gain access to the Litani River are revealed in the pages of Moshe Sharett's personal diary. Head of the Jewish Agency's Political Department from 1933 to 1948, Sharett became Israel's first foreign minister in 1949 under David Ben-Gurion. In 1954 he served as Prime Minister when Ben-Gurion retired. When Ben-Gurion returned to public life, Sharett yielded the post of Prime Minister to him but remained Foreign Minister until June 1956. Excerpts from his diary, a two-thousand-four-hundred-page document in eight volumes, were translated in 1978 from Hebrew to English by an Italian writer and journalist, Livia Rokach.

Sharett's diary entry for February 27, 1954 recounts an important meeting with Ben-Gurion, Defense Minister Pinhas Lavon and Chief of Staff Moshe Dayan shortly after a coup d'etat in Syria. Ben-Gurion insisted, and Levon and Dayan agreed, that "this is the time to arouse Lebanon – that is to say the Maronites – to proclaim a Christian State." Sharett opposed the idea insisting the Maronites were divided and not interested.

Ben-Gurion countered that the Maronites could be made to accept the idea. "We'll send envoys and spend money and if there is no money, we will find it ... For such a project, it is worthwhile throwing away one hundred thousand, half a million, a million dollars."[77]

The next day Ben-Gurion tried again to convince Sharett. "Perhaps now is the time to bring about the creation of a Christian State in our neighborhood. Without our initiative and our vigorous aid this will not be done. It seems to me that this is the central duty – or at least one of the central duties of our foreign policy. This means that time, energy and means ought to be invested in it and that we must act in all possible ways to bring about a radical change in Lebanon. We must concentrate all our efforts on this issue ... This is a historical opportunity. Missing it will be unpardonable."[78]

....

77 Rokach, Livia. *Israel's Sacred Terrorism*, Chapter 5, pp. 1–2.
78 Randall, Jonathan. Ibid. pp. 190–191.

Sharett pondered two weeks before replying: "There is no point or purpose in trying to create from the outside a movement which is nonexistent inside. One can reinforce a spirit of life when it is already beating. One cannot inject life into a body which shows no sign of life … There is no movement today in Lebanon seeking to make that country a Christian state in which the final word would be in the hands of the Maronite community."[79]

Sharett's reasonableness did not persuade either Ben-Gurion or his close advisors to drop plans to destabilize Lebanon. More than a year later, at a staff meeting on May 15, 1955, Moshe Dayan went so far as to suggest that "all that is needed is to find an officer, even a major. We should win his heart or buy him, to get him to agree to declare himself the savior of the Maronite population. Then the Israeli Army would enter Lebanon, occupy the necessary territory to acquire the Litani River and set up a Christian regime allied to Israel and everything will turn out just fine."[80]

In his diary Sharett lamented the military's "simply appalling lack of seriousness in its whole approach to neighboring countries." He wrote: "I see clearly how those who served Israel with their heroism and sacrifice in the War of Independence are capable of bringing catastrophe on it if they are allowed a free hand in normal times."[81]

These excerpts from Sharett's diary make uncanny reading in light of what has happened in Lebanon since 1975. Civil war *did* envelop Lebanon. Israel *did* latch onto a renegade Christian army officer by the name of Major Saad Haddad, who *did* do Israel's bidding in South Lebanon. The Western powers *did* go along with Lebanon's effective dismemberment, although less to save the threatened Christians than out of lassitude.[82] And Israel *did* attempt in each of its invasions to reach, so as to control, the Litani River.

....

79 Ibid.
80 Ibid, p. 193.
81 Ibid, p. 194.
82 Ibid.

The issue of water, or the lack thereof, is an urgent one for Israel. Historically, any analysis of the conflict between Israel and the Palestinians has focused on religious differences. This is a shallow veneer covering a deeper conflict for this much more basic resource. When war did in fact break out in 1967, the water issue was among major Israeli concerns in launching a preemptive attack. With purposeful planning, Israeli tanks and troops stationed across the proposed route effectively completed Israel's encirclement of the headwaters of the Upper Jordan, which include the West Bank. Its seizure of Syria's Golan Heights assured Israeli protection for the Lake Tiberias (Sea of Galilee) pumping works while the take-over of Gaza gave Israel plentiful water supplies.[83] These territories have proven very problematic but the precious water it afforded Israel has far outweighed the diplomatic cost of its forty-year military occupation.[84]

Israel's ecology varies from semi-arid to complete desert, yet it has intense water needs. These are fulfilled primarily by three sources. The Sea of Galilee provides over a third of Israel's water. Another third comes from two aquifers – large, geographical areas of subterranean catchments where water accumulates. These lie beneath the Gaza Strip and the West Bank, precisely the territories Israel seized in the 1967 war.[85]

Under international law, the West Bank and Gaza are occupied territories and the Geneva Conventions forbid moving people into an occupied territory. However, this is exactly what Israel's settlement program did. Israel then proceeded to siphon the water of the West Bank away from its native Palestinian population to the new settler population. Currently, Israelis in the West Bank receive 92.5 gallons per person per day while Palestinians get 18.5 gallons per person per day. The minimum amount recommended by the

· ·

83 Schmida, Leslie C. "Israel's Drive for Water," *The Link*, Volume 17, Issue 4, Americans for Middle East Understanding, November 1984. www.ameu.org

84 Godesky, Jason. "Israel's Water Wars." *The Anthropik Network*, August 15, 2006. http://anthropik.com/2006/08/israels-water-wars

85 Ibid.

World Health Organization for household and urban use is 26.4 gallons per day per person.[86]

Since August 1982 the Israelis have drilled at least three new wells in the West Bank – deep bore holes from three to six hundred meters deep that pump an estimated fifteen to seventeen million cubic meters (MCM) annually – for their sole usage.[87] No Palestinian since 1967 has received permission to drill a new irrigation well for agricultural purposes, and less than ten new wells for domestic Palestinian consumption have been authorized. [88]

In August 2005 one of the reasons then-Prime Minister Ariel Sharon withdrew Israeli settlers from the Gaza Strip was because it had ceased to provide the water it once had. The level of salt and other pollutants had reduced the quality in numerous sites to below what was permissible for drinking water. Once Israel had used up the resources and it was no longer potable, Sharon gave up the cost of defending the Strip and returned it to the Palestinians.[89]

While the 1967 war helped Israel secure eighty to eighty-five percent of the West Bank's water, its new Separation Wall ensures yet another means of claiming even more water. An article in *Haaretz* estimated that the bizarre loops and zigzags of the Separation Wall, adhering to no previous delineation, and not even remotely resembling the pre-'67 border, placed ninety-five percent of the aquifers on the Israeli side.[90]

Israel's voracious consumption and lack of environmental responsibility has turned its water problem into a crisis. To continue its growth, Israel needs new sources of water, by any means necessary.

For decades, Israel has seen permanent occupation of South

....

86 Godesky, Jason.

87 Awartani, Hisham. "Water Resources and Policies in the West Bank." *Samed el-Iqtisadi*, Vol. 3, August 1980, p.6.

88 Sahliyeh, Emile. "West Bank Industrial and Agricultural Development: The Basic Problems." *Journal of Palestine Studies* XI: 2, Winter 1982, p. 66.

89 Godesky, Jason.

90 Ibid.

Lebanon and continued access to the Litani River as the answer to its water problem. Such an acquisition would increase the annual water supply of Israel by up to eight hundred MCM, or approximately forty percent of its current annual water consumption.

The 170-kilometer-long Litani River, with its 2,290 square kilometer basin, is located entirely within the borders of Lebanon. The river rises in the central part of the northern Bekaa Valley, a short distance west of Baalbeck, and flows between the Lebanon Mountains to the west and the Anti-Lebanon mountains to the east. It continues southwest toward Nabatiya and the Beaufort Castle where it abruptly turns west to flow through the hilly terrain of the al-Amal region, north of Tyre before emptying in the Mediterranean.[91] The river's proximity to Israel, a distance of some four kilometers, makes it even more tempting for Israel to exploit.

Another attraction of the Litani River is the high quality of its water. The salinity level is only twenty parts per million whereas that of the Sea of Galilee is 250 to 350 parts per million. Such water quality could help repair the water sources that Israel's overuse has turned salty and brackish.[92]

In a 1920 letter to Prime Minister David Lloyd George, Chaim Weizmann, then head of the World Zionist Organization (WZO), argued that Lebanon was "well watered" and that the river was "valueless to the territory north of Israel's proposed frontiers. They can be used more beneficially in the country further south." Weizmann concluded that the WZO considered the Litani valley "for a distance of twenty-five miles above the bend" of the river essential to the future of the Jewish "national home." The British and French mandate powers disregarded this recommendation and retained the Litani basin entirely in Lebanon.[93]

....

91   Moss, Angela Joy. "Litani River and Israel-Lebanon." *ICE Case Studies: Litani River Dispute.* www.american.edu/ted/ice/litani.htm

92   Amery, Hussein A. "The Litani River of Lebanon." *Geographical Review,* Vol. 83, Issue 3, p. 229, July 1993.

93   Weisgal, M.W., ed. "The Letters and Papers of Chaim Weizmann." Vol. 9. Jerusalem, Israel Universities Press, 1977.

The water sources captured in 1967 were estimated to last Israel only into the 1980s. Israel hoped to meet its additional water needs when it invaded South Lebanon in 1978 in what it called "Operation Litani." The official excuse was to create a "security zone" in South Lebanon to better protect its own northern border. Shortly after establishing the security zone, a US military observer witnessed Israeli soldiers burying pipes deep in the ground near Marjayoun, probably used to siphon underground water from an aquifer fed by seepage from the Litani and by underground streams from Mt. Hermon.[94] Any increase in overall Israeli water supply cannot be verified, however, for Israel has not published full water or cultivation figures since 1978.[95]

Immediately after the 1982 invasion, the Israeli Army stationed two battalions along the northeastern shore of Lake Karaoun (in the Bekaa Valley) and seized all hydrographic charts and technical documents relating to the Litani. In January 1983 the Israelis conducted seismic sounding and engaged in construction activity near the Litani, only three miles from the nearest water source in Israel. Israeli officials have confirmed these activities.[96]

On August 29, 1984, Lebanese Representative to the UN Rashid Fakhoury reported to the United Nations Security Council that the engineering branch of the Israeli Military of Defense spent the latter half of August 1984 digging a three-kilometer-long tunnel from Deir Mimas on the Litani River to Kfar Kila close to the Israeli border – a tunnel large enough to accommodate sufficient flow of the Litani River into Israel[97] and deliver Israel an additional five hundred MCM annually, thereby reducing the amount of water available to Lebanese farmers.[98]

....

94 Cooley, John K. "The War over Water." *Foreign Policy* No. 54, Spring 1984, p. 23.

95 Schmida, Leslie C.

96 Ibid.

97 "Provisional Verbatim Record of the Two Thousand Five Hundred and Fifty-Second Meetings." United Nations Security Council, *S/PV*, 2552, August 30, 1984.

98 Stauffer, Thomas R. "Water and War in the Middle East: the Hydraulic Parameters of Conflict." *Information Paper Number 5*, The Center for Policy Analysis on Palestine, Washington, D.C., July 1996.

At the same time Israeli Defense Forces began to fence off a number of public and private properties and prohibited fishing in the river and other civilian activity. Marjayoun area farmers complained that they were forbidden by the Israeli Army from digging any new wells.[99]

Other important water sources are the Hasbani River and its tributary, the Wazzani, which supply twenty to twenty-five percent of the water flowing into the Sea of Galilee (Lake Tiberias), feeding Israel's water supply. The Hasbani rises in Lebanon and flows for about fifty kilometers through Lebanese territory before joining the Jordan River and emptying into the Sea of Galilee.[100]

The Wazzani starts off as the Hasbani River and flows under an elegant Roman bridge below Mount Hermon and the occupied Golan Heights. Then its name changes to the Wazzani and meanders below Ghajar, a village split between Lebanon and the Israeli-occupied Golan Heights, trickles into Israel, fills up the Kibbutzim fish lakes and ends up in the Jordan River before feeding Lake Tiberias, which is Israel's prime source of drinking water.[101]

Israel destroyed Lebanon's original pumping station and eight-inch pipe located beside the Wazzani Springs during the 1967 war, denying Lebanon the use of the spring water for thirty-nine years.[102]

On August 14, 1984, the Israeli newspaper *Haaretz* reported that Tahal, the Israeli water planning authority, had devised a means of diverting Hasbani water to Israel via the defunct Tapline oil pipeline which once transported oil from Saudi Arabia to Jor-

....

99   "L'Etat Hebreu s' Appreterait a Detourner Les Eaux du Hasbani." *Orient-LeJour*, Agence France-Presse, August 14, 1984.

100 "Lebanon: Rivers Form Part of the Conflict with Israel." August 25, 2006. www.irc. nl/page/30506

101 Fisk, Robert. "Water War Looms as Israel Tells Lebanon to Halt River Works." *The Independent*, September 26, 2002.

102 Blanford, Nicholas. "Heightened Israeli-Lebanese Tensions over Jordan's Headwaters." *Middle East Report*, September 30, 2002. www.merip.org/mero/ mero093002.html

dan, Syria and Lebanon.[103] Whether or not this scheme was actually carried out cannot be verified. However, it is likely that the buried pipes installed by the Israeli Army in 1978 are being used to siphon underground water from the Hasbani River.

A major crisis erupted in August 2002 when the Council of the South began a water-pumping project at the Wazzani Springs. The plan entailed pumping some ten thousand cubic meters of water per day from the springs and conveying it via a sixteen-inch pipe to a reservoir near a village six miles west of the Wazzani. Up to sixty villages in the border area would be supplied with drinking water. Then-Israeli Prime Minister Ariel Sharon announced that the scheme represented a "casus belli."[104] Israeli officials traveled to Washington and New York to complain of Lebanon's plans to "divert" the Wazzani. Lebanon, however, insisted that it was entitled to draw water from the Wazzani and the Hasbani Rivers and vowed that the scheme would proceed. Under international law the Lebanese may pump thirty-five MCM of water a year and they intended to pump only twelve MCM. Other statistics suggest that the Lebanese already pump seven MCM further north and intend only to raise this figure to nine MCM.[105]

This brings us to the 2006 war with Hezbollah and Israel's attempt, once again, to establish a "security buffer" to protect its northern border. In light of the evidence already presented, it is conceivable that the war was not as much about protecting Israel's northern border and defeating Hezbollah as it was about gaining access to the Litani River. Historically Hezbollah has been primarily a nuisance to Israel, never a genuine threat to its survival, unlike Israel's lack of access to the Litani.

The Lebanese government is under extreme pressure not to give in to Israel's demands for water. Such an action would precipitate a new Lebanese crisis. Diverting the Litani would stunt

····················

103 *L'Orient-LeJour*, Agence France-Press, August 14, 1984.
104 Blanford, Nicholas.
105 Fisk, Robert.

the economic development of the country, frustrate the postwar nation-building process and strengthen the hands of groups calling for the cantonization or Islamization of the country. Without the Litani waters, irrigation would be virtually impossible in the south and much of the region would become desert. Denying the Shia of South Lebanon water for domestic and agricultural uses would aggravate even more their frustrations with the central government.

Lebanon is blessed with average annual rainfall in excess of eight hundred MCM. In Mount Lebanon and Anti-Lebanon that helps sustain more than two thousand springs during the seven-month dry season. However, climate changes are already taking its toll on Lebanon's water resources. The year 2006 was one of its driest precipitation seasons ever, and with agricultural and population demands continuing to grow, the decades-long misuse and underuse of existing resources likely means that Lebanon will face a severe water crisis, perhaps as early as 2010.[106]

The Lebanese government finally began to take ameliorative action in 1999-2000 by passing a series of statutory reforms. More recently the Decennial Plan (2001–2010) has been put forward. It calls for over $1.5 billion in new spending on refurbishing the aging network, capacity expansion, including more than thirty new dams, water mains and pumping stations. The plan, spearheaded by Fadi Comair, Director General of Hydraulic and Electrical Resources, will require major funding. Only about $80 million have been spent so far, leaving more than $900 million in yet-to-be-funded projects that are vital for ensuring the future functioning of Lebanon's water network.[107]

A simple solution to the water crisis has existed since at least 1949 when then-Syrian President Hosni Zaim proposed a peace treaty with Israel in which he offered to *share* the waters of the Sea

....

106 Long, William. "Water Reform Efforts Stuck In Neutral as Crisis Looms." *The Daily Star*, August 20, 2007.

107 Ibid.

of Galilee. Israel refused. In 2007 Syrian President Bachar Assad offered a revised version of the 1949 peace treaty, based on the 1955 Johnston Plan, which offered another formula for *sharing* the water resources of the Sea of Galilee. Israel refused to ratify the proposal.

According to Fadi Comair, this is a huge problem since it centers on the very heart of the matter – the *equitable use* of water and reasonable *sharing*.[108]

SHEBAA FARMS

The Shebaa Farms is a water-rich area some fourteen square miles in size. This agricultural area consists of fourteen farms located south of Shebaa, a Lebanese village on the western slopes of Mount Hermon, at a corner where Syria, Lebanon and Israel meet. The region remained under Israeli control after the withdrawal of Israeli forces from South Lebanon in 2000. Israel administers it as part of the Golan Heights, which it officially annexed in 1981. Both Lebanese and Syrian officials insisted that Syria had officially given the territory to Lebanon in 1951. Lebanese officials point to the fact that a number of residents in the area have land deeds stamped by the Lebanese government, yet Israel insisted the territory belonged to Syria and could only be negotiated in a formal peace treaty between Israel and Syria.

The abundance of water in the Shebaa Farms area comes mainly from precipitation. Although the rate of evaporation is as high as fifty to fifty-five percent, the geological formations in the Mount Hermon-Shebaa Farms area allow the formation of major underground reservoirs.[109] The geology belongs to the Jurassic age and its rocks are characterized by their fissured karstic limestone that allows the infiltration of water into the underground layers. The gradual melting of snow during the warm seasons further

....

108 Ibid.
109 "Shebaa Has Key Water Resources." *The Daily Star*, April 5, 2001.

enriches the ground water and increases the number of springs and water courses at lower elevations, such as that found in the Shebaa Farms area.

Mount Hermon serves as an important source of surface water for the Hasbani River, located near the southern part of the Shebaa Farms inside Lebanon and a tributary of the Jordan River inside Israel. It is in the area of the Shebaa Farms that Israeli engineers have installed pipes to pump hundreds of cubic meters of water directly into Israel.[110]

According to Nasser Nasrallah, Director-General of the Litani River Authority, "The amount of groundwater which moves across the border to Israel from the Lebanese side in an average year is two hundred MCM, 113 million of which comes from the Shebaa Farms and the groundwater of the Hasbani River and Wazzani Springs." Of the 113 MCM, the groundwater of the Hasbani River and the Wazzani Springs account for fifty-five MCM while the remaining fifty-eight MCM flows from the Shebaa Farms area.[111] Lebanon's water rights to the Hasbani, which have been lost since 1969, are 1.5 billion cubic meters. The price of each cubic meter is fifty cents. Additional losses stem from Israel preventing Lebanon from irrigating five thousand hectares of Lebanese land which led to a lack of investment in the area.[112]

According to Nasrallah, the direct and indirect losses in regard to rights in the Hasbani River amount to over $2 billion. Nasrallah also has information that Israel has dug wells to extract as much groundwater as possible. "They are using so much groundwater that some of the permanent Lebanese springs near the borders with Israel, like the Marj al-Khokh spring, dry up in the summer."[113]

. . .

....

110 Ibid.
111 Ibid.
112 Ibid.
113 Ibid.

The other issue with the Shebaa Farms is political in nature.

During the 1967 war Israeli forces seized the Shebaa Farms. Since Lebanon was not a participant in the war, they had no voice and the UN representatives were pressured by Israel, who falsely claimed that the 1923 Anglo-French demarcation and the 1949 Armistice line designated the area as Syrian territory.[114]

When Israel ended its twenty-two-year occupation of South Lebanon in May 2000, it kept control of the Shebaa Farms area, claiming it was Syrian, to be returned when both countries signed a peace treaty. Hezbollah, certain the territory belonged to Lebanon, maintained that as long as Israel continued to occupy this tiny piece of land, it would not relinquish its arms.

On July 18, 2000, under intense pressure from the United States, the UN Security Council affixed its imprimatur to the proposition that Israel, after its occupation of South Lebanon, finally complied with the provisions of UN Resolution 424 and ended its illegal occupation. Had no further fuss been made about the Shebaa Farms, we would have assumed that Israel, in fact, had fulfilled its obligations and had withdrawn from all Lebanese territory.[115]

Under apparent pressure from the White House, the UN remained mute on the question of the Shebaa Farms for six years. On July 11, 2007, however, UN Secretary-General Ban Ki-Moon certified that the Shebaa Farms area was Lebanese, not Syrian, and that Israel still occupied Lebanese territory, a claim Hezbollah has repeatedly made.[116] Ban's office invited the Israelis to withdraw immediately. Israel objected saying that its own recently retained cartographers needed to open the whole border dispute question from the beginning and examine all the work and findings of the UN map experts. Such a revised map review process would take years "to do right" according to a legal brief filed by Alan Dershowitz, a Harvard law professor. Since both Syria and Lebanon

....

114 Lamb, Franklin. "Lebanon's Shebaa Farms." *CounterPunch*, July 17, 2007. http://counterpunch.org/lamb07172007.html

115 Ibid.

116 Ibid.

agreed on Lebanon's ownership of the Shebaa Farms, the filing of any legal brief would appear unnecessary.[117]

As soon as the news was made public Israel's Foreign Minister, Tzipi Livni, contacted the White House and demanded it act to reverse the UN decision. Following the White House's intervention, Secretary-General Ban, in an abrupt turnaround, issued a statement insisting that, after further consideration, any decision on the ownership of the Shebaa Farms was premature. "I have submitted my report on this issue. My senior cartographer has made some good progress but this report does not appear to mention anything about ownership or sovereignty yet. The UN's cartographer continues his work and will be visiting the area shortly."[118]

Whether the UN Secretary-General ultimately does the right thing and declares officially that the Shebaa Farms do indeed belong to Lebanon remains to be seen. If he chooses, for reasons of job security, to ignore the evidence, it will not be the first time a UN Secretary-General has been made to bend to Washington's demands.

The Shebaa Farms, in the end, presents the Bush administration with an unusual dilemma.

If the UN eventually declares that the Shebaa Farms area belongs to Lebanon, this decision will bestow international legitimacy on Hezbollah and its steadfast resistance to Israel's occupation of the Shebaa Farms. Hezbollah will then claim another victory over Israel, thereby gaining more credibility throughout the Arab world.

On the other hand, Israel's withdrawal from the Shebaa Farms would strengthen the Siniora government because it could then legitimately call on Hezbollah to disarm. President Bush desperately needs such a boost to keep his regional policies on life support.[119]

· · ·

· ·

117 Ibid.
118 Ibid.
119 Ibid.

Israel, if it can muster the requisite attitude and political will, has a clear choice on the vital issue of water. In the occupied territories, it can cease its unilateral confiscation of the common water resources and yield to the Palestinians their fair share in accordance with international law. By so doing, Israel would not suffer appreciable harm because it already possesses greater quantities of water than the Palestinians to meet its baseline needs. It has superior economic and technical capabilities to tap rich alternative water resources. It also has a broad sea front on the Mediterranean, which affords it practically limitless amounts of water for desalinization technology that it already sells worldwide.[120]

Lebanon's Litani River, on the other hand, cannot and should not be shared. It is essential for the country's agriculture and industrial development. The river also provides thirty-five percent of the country's total production of electricity.

The Hasbani River and the Wazzani Springs could, on the other hand, be equitably shared by both Lebanon and Israel, if the latter agrees to such an arrangement. In the end, however, Israel must realize that nothing is gained through menacing threats and military incursions. Rather, security and lasting peace are achieved through diplomacy and respect of the other's water rights and needs.

....

120 Moss, Angela Joy. "Litani River and Israel-Lebanon." *ICE Case Studies: Litani River Dispute*. www.american.edu/ted/ice/litani.htm

8

NEW WORRIES:
THE PALESTINIANS AND
FATAH AL-ISLAM

Of the original sixteen Palestinian refugee camps in Lebanon set up to settle the more than one hundred thousand refugees crossing the Israeli border in '47–48, only twelve camps remain. Many Palestinians in the camp of Tal el-Za-atar were massacred by Christian militias in 1976 during Lebanon's civil war, and the rest were forcibly removed. Three additional camps were destroyed by Israeli air attacks during their '82 invasion and by other Lebanese militia. The remaining twelve camps now house the majority of Lebanon's 433,276 refugees.[121]

One such camp is Nahr al-Bared, located seven miles north of Tripoli in northern Lebanon along the Mediterranean. It is home to some thirty-two thousand refugees, many of whom were expelled from northern Galilee when the State of Israel was established in '48. Twenty-five percent of Nahr al-Bared residents live in abject poverty, which is defined by Lebanon's National Millennium Development Goal Report as expenditure of less than $1.30 per day. Compared to Syria, Jordan and the other Arab countries who have hosted Palestinian refugees since 1948, Lebanon has the

....

121 Lamb, Franklin. "Who's Behind the Fighting in North Lebanon." *Counterpunch*, May 24, 2007.

89

worst human rights record toward its Palestinian refugees. They are denied citizenship, banned from working in seventy trades and professions and cannot own real estate. They have no access to public social services and rely solely on the United Nations for their most basic needs.[122] Like most of the other camps, Nahr al-Bared also suffers from lack of proper water, sewage and electricity.

On May 20, 2007, a battle broke out inside this impoverished camp.

The simple version of events says a group of men robbed a bank in Amyoun on the outskirts of Tripoli on May 19 and, pursued by police, fled inside the Nahr al-Bared camp. The Lebanese Army, because it patrols the perimeters of the camp, found itself embroiled in a fight with an unknown Sunni militant group calling itself Fatah al-Islam.

As with everything in Lebanon, the story is more complicated than just a simple bank robbery. In fact, it actually begins with an article in *The New Yorker* by investigative journalist Seymour Hersh entitled "The Redirection." When initial news reports of Nahr al-Bared mentioned Sunni al-Qaeda-linked insurgents, I re-read the Hersh article with renewed interest. American policy in the Middle East, according to Hersh, had shifted to opposing Iran, Syria and their Shiite ally, Hezbollah, at any cost, even if it meant backing hard-line Sunni militants. A key element of this policy shift was an agreement among Vice President Dick Cheney, Deputy National Security Advisor Elliott Abrams and Prince Bandar bin Sultan, the Saudi National Security Advisor (linked along with Elliott Abrams to the Iran-Contra scandal), whereby the Saudis would covertly fund the Sunni insurgents in Lebanon as a counterweight to the Shiite Hezbollah. The assassination of Hassan Nasrallah was also part of the plan. Hersh explained that even though the United States appeared to be acting in a way counter to its interests, when the Israelis lost the war to Hezbollah, "the fear of Hezbollah in Washington, particularly in the White House, became acute."[123]

....

122 Ibid.

123 Hersh, Seymour. "The Redirection." *The New Yorker*, March 5, 2007.

By May 23rd many Beirut-based journalists started to make the connections, too, and began filling in the details about Fatah al-Islam, a group of some four hundred insurgents from Saudi Arabia, Pakistan, Algeria, Iraq and Tunisia who had arrived in Nahr al-Bared in October 2006.

Their leader is Shaker al-Absi, an associate of the infamous al-Qaeda-linked insurgent Abu Musab al-Zarqawi. Absi served many years in a Syrian jail and was sentenced to death in absentia in Jordan in 2004 for the 2002 murder of US diplomat Laurence Foley. Since Absi served time in Syria, many Lebanese politicians, Saad Hariri in particular, pointed the finger at Syria, blaming it for events in Nahr al-Bared. However, Syria is a secular regime and hates the al-Qaeda-linked extremists. In February 1982, the President's late father, Hafez al-Assad, killed ten thousand members of the Sunni radical group the Muslim Brotherhood in Hama. According to Robert Fisk, Assad suspected the Israelis were involved in creating this particular branch of the radical group.[124]

The Lebanese government's version of events, nonetheless, casts Fatah al-Islam as characters in the latest installment in a saga of Syrian meddling in Lebanon, intended to remind the Lebanese of Damascus' indispensable role in maintaining Lebanese security.[125] Lebanese journalist Michael Young also claims that Syria is responsible for Fatah al-Islam because it seeks to undermine the proposed UN Hariri tribunal and wants a decisive say in who becomes Lebanon's next president. According to Young, the Assad regime never reconciled itself with its forced withdrawal from Lebanon and is now actively seeking to reimpose its hegemony over its neighbor through a network of allies and agents.[126] Another wrinkle in this story to counter the Syrian conspiracy theory is the apparent complicity of the Hariri family in this affair. At the very

....

124 Fisk, Robert. *Pity the Nation: The Abduction of Lebanon.* Antheneum, New York, 1990, p. 181.

125 Quilty, Jim. "The Collateral Damage of Lebanese Sovereignty." MERIP, June 18, 2007. http://www.merip.org/mero/mero061807.html

126 Young, Michael. "Destruction and Deceit in Northern Lebanon." *The Daily Star*, May 24, 2007.

least they gambled on a scheme hatched by the Bush administration and lost when their involvement became public knowledge. According to investigative journalist and international lawyer Franklin Lamb, who reported on these events from inside Nahr al-Bared, a plan was devised following the death of Rafic Hariri to create a US-supported Sunni Army of the North to counter the Iran-supported Shiite Army in the South. The scheme was flawed from the start because it required igniting a civil war between Lebanon's Muslims and Christians, between Sunni and Shiite, between Palestinians and Lebanese. So far, at least, the scheme has failed.[127]

After Rafic Hariri was assassinated in February 2006, the Hariri family no longer trusted the existing state security and intelligence forces, so with supervision and funding from the US and Saudi Arabia, they established their own quasi-militia called the Lebanese Internal Security Forces. They also established something called Jihaz al-Ma'alumat, the intelligence apparatus, which does not have a mandate to exist under Lebanese law.

Again, according to Franklin Lamb, the Supreme Sunni Grand Mufti Mohammed Kabbani stands accused of acting on orders from Saad Hariri to arrange as many as 250 "religious scholar visas" from the government of Lebanon for devout persons from Saudi Arabia and elsewhere. The accusation is that these visas facilitated the legal entrance into Lebanon over the past nine months of al-Qaeda fighters who joined Fatah al-Islam.[128]

In 2005, according to the International Crisis Group, Saad Hariri paid $48,000 in bail for four members of an Islamic militant group accused of trying to establish an Islamic mini-state in northern Lebanon. The Crisis Group said that these militants had

....

127 Lamb, Franklin. "Writing from Bibnin Akkar, opposite Nahr al-Bared." *People's Geography – Reclaiming Space*. http://peoplesgeography.com/2007/06/02/lamb-lebanese-army-enter-nahr-al-bared-june-1/

128 Ibid.

trained in al-Qaeda camps in Afghanistan."[129] Saad Hariri, according to the Crisis Group, also used his parliamentary majority to obtain amnesty for twenty-two other militants as well as for seven insurgents suspected of plotting to bomb the Italian and Ukrainian embassies in Beirut.[130]

Alastair Crooke, who spent nearly thirty years in MI6, the British intelligence service, and now works with Conflicts Forum, a think tank in Beirut, told Hersh that "the Lebanese government is opening space for these people to come in. The Sunni extremist group, Fatah al-Islam, splintered from another extremist group. Within twenty-four hours they were being offered weapons and money by people presenting themselves as representatives of the Lebanese government's interests, presumably to take on Hezbollah."[131]

While no evidence has been presented to prove categorically Hariri's entanglement with Fatah al-Islam, the theory, according to Jim Quilty, is not entirely baseless either. The Hariri family's relationship with Sunni Islamism goes back to the start of Lebanon's 2005 parliamentary elections when Saad Hariri spent lavishly to support his Future Movement list, including payment to some of the extremist Islamist groups in the north. In March 2007, Bahiyya al-Hariri, Saad's aunt and member of Parliament, was caught paying thousands of dollars to Islamists to leave the Ayn al-Hilwa Palestinian camp in Sidon in South Lebanon, only they did not leave.[132]

On June 3, clashes broke out between the Lebanese Army and insurgents inside the Ayn al-Hilwa camp. Insurgents taken into custody on June 12 confessed that they had a "hit list" with some thirty names. Walid Eido, a Deputy who had been assassinated two days earlier, was on that list, as were the UNIFIL soldiers stationed

....

129 Hersh, Seymour.
130 Ibid.
131 Ibid.
132 Quilty, Jim.

along the Israeli-Lebanese border. It was eerily unsettling, then, when on July 4 Fatah al-Islam insurgents were linked to a roadside bombing that killed six UN peacekeepers. Three Spaniards and three Colombians died in the blast, which struck their personnel carrier as they patrolled the main road between the towns of Marjayoun and Khiam near the Israeli border.

. . .

Meanwhile, in the north the plan began to unravel when Hezbollah's intelligence found out about the Hariri-funded insurgents. Saad Hariri then stopped the flow of money to Fatah al-Islam's account at the Hariri-owned bank near Tripoli. Angry, the insurgents robbed the bank. Hariri then ordered his Internal Security Forces to attack the group in their apartments in Tripoli. The Hariri forces were unsuccessful and the insurgents fled to Nahr al-Bared. The Siniora cabinet convened in an emergency session and asked the Lebanese Army to enter the refugee camp and eliminate Fatah al-Islam. Press reports stated that the Lebanese Army was prevented from entering the camp because of a secret agreement struck between the Lebanese Army and the PLO in Cairo in 1969. Known as the Cairo Agreement, the document authorized Palestinian Armed Struggle, a security arm of the PLO to "undertake the task of regulating and determining the presence of arms in the camps within the framework of Lebanese security and the interests of the Palestinian revolution." What the press failed to report in this story was that the agreement was officially rescinded by the Lebanese parliament on May 21, 1987, exactly twenty years before clashes erupted in Nahr al-Bared. So why did the Army not enter the camp? According to Muhammad Ali Khalidi and Diane Riskedahl, the answer is quite complex. "Arguably, in the fragmented quasi-state that is post-war Lebanon, it suits the interests of various groups to maintain pockets of the country that can be blamed for outbreaks of instability. Different factions can use them to foment unrest, while maintaining 'plausible deniability' that they are the instigators of the disturbances. The losers in this dangerous political game are primarily the Palestinian refugees themselves."[133] Franklin Lamb also suggests that were the Army to enter one of the camps such an act would open up a front against the Army in all twelve Palestinian camps, tearing the army apart along sectarian lines. The majority of Lebanese soldiers are Shiite while the Palestinians in these camps are Sunni.[134] The Army, for its part, felt set up by Hariri's Internal Security Forces because it did not make the Army aware of its relations with Fatah al-Islam. The Army, because of this slight, could not warn its soldiers posted outside the Nahr al-Bared camp of the Fatah al-Islam insurgents.

When the insurgents assaulted the Lebanese soldiers at the camp's entrance, the Army responded by cutting off water and electricity and pounding the camp with tank, artillery and heavy machine gun fire. The refugees inside the camp got no warning of an impending assault and the result was a humanitarian crisis. Four days into the camp battle, two-thirds of the Palestinians were finally able to leave. Many sought shelter in the nearby Baddawi camp.[135]

For the besieged Palestinians who survived repeated destruction and sieges of their camps during Lebanon's civil war, this latest crisis brought back painful memories. The fear too is that their plight will be completely drowned out by the paeans to the Lebanese army, whose symbolic power as the repository of pined-for national unity has long been greater than its combat effectiveness. When the fighting finally ended on September 10, 2007, the Army had lost 165 men.

Some fear there may be an even more sinister plot afoot. Former President Amine Gemayel explicitly wed the camps to al-Qaeda, suggesting the presence of "evil terrorist forces" neces-

....

133 Khalidi, Muhammad Ali and Diane Riskedahl. "The Road to Nahr al-Bared: Lebanese Political Discourse and Palestinian Civil Rights." *Middle East Report*, Number 244, Fall 2007, pp. 26–33.

134 Lamb, Franklin. "Who's Behind the Fighting in North Lebanon."

135 Quilty, Jim.

sitated the "cleansing of the camps." "No matter how much the Palestinians may deny their relationship with these destructive elements," said Gemayel, "the certain truth is that they have found themselves a place inside the camps without Palestinian opposition." Such remarks raise questions in Palestinian circles about the means Lebanon and its Western allies might employ to implement the disarmament of "non-Lebanese militias," such as the Palestinians, called for in UN Resolution 1559. Upon leaving Nahr al-Bared, one displaced Palestinian refugee reported a Lebanese soldier promising that the army would soon clean out all the camps in exactly this manner.[136]

The "cleansing of the camps" rhetoric brings up the final wrinkle in this tragic story that centers on an abandoned airbase at Kleiaat next to Nahr al-Bared. It is here that the Bush administration wants to build a US air base. To make the project more palatable, according to Franklin Lamb, it is being promoted as a US/NATO base that will serve as the headquarters of a NATO rapid deployment force.

Lebanese entrepreneurs loyal to Hariri in the north will be the chief financial winners from the project with thousands of new construction jobs coming their way. The people who will not benefit from the building boom will be the Palestinians from Nahr al-Bared, which is literally next door to the anticipated project. These refugees, who were driven from their homes in Palestine in '48 and '67, from parts of Lebanon in '75, '78, '82, '93, '96 and 2006, will gain no work from Kleiaat because, as already stated, the seventy top trades and professions in Lebanon are denied to Palestinians under Lebanese law.[137] A Lebanese journalist who opposes the base commented to Franklin Lamb on May 28, 2007 that "the Bush administration has been warning Lebanon about the pres-

....

136 Ibid.

137 Lamb, Franklin. "It's the US Air Base, Stupid." *People's Geography – Reclaiming Space.* http://www.peoplesgeography.com/2007/05/30/latest-franklin-lamb-on-lebanon-its-the-us-airbase-stupid/

ence of al-Qaeda teams in northern Lebanon. And the base is needed to deal with this threat. Low and behold, a new terrorist group called Fatah al-Islam appears near Kleiaat at the Nahr al-Bared camp."[138]

The Pentagon argues that the military base will contribute to the development and the economic recovery in the region and advises the Lebanese government to focus on the financial aspect and positive reflection on the ninety-five percent Sunni population in the region.

....

138 Ibid.

THE MEDIA'S COVERAGE
OF THE WAR

MYTHS VERSUS REALITY

As someone who lived in Lebanon for fourteen years, eight of
which were during Lebanon's civil war, I am particularly sensitive
to how conflicts are covered, especially those that involve Lebanon
and Israel. I am also keenly aware that accusations of anti-Semitism are frequently used to silence any discussion of Israel and its
military actions. I declare, therefore, before I begin this section of
the book, that any criticism against the State of Israel is directed
at its political and military actions during the 2006 war, and not
against Judaism. Hezbollah is an organic Shiite Lebanese political and military movement and any criticism against its behavior
during the war is not against Shiite Islam or Islam in general. That
said, since both Israel and Hezbollah are guilty of war crimes, it is
reasonable and necessary to have an honest and frank discussion
about their conduct and how the media covered it.

To begin, let me dispel several myths that distract from the
facts:

1. **Israel's very existence was at stake.** No, Israel's existence
was not at stake and has not been for decades, if it ever was. It
has the second largest fleet of F-16s on the planet, second only to
the United States, and is the single largest recipient of foreign aid
since the early '70s, receiving close to $3 billion annually, seventy-

five percent of which must be spent to buy weapons from the US military industrial complex.

Perhaps a better question would be: Can Israel successfully invade another country such as Lebanon, conduct a conventional war against a homegrown guerrilla movement that knows the terrain like the back of its hand and win? No, chances are Israel would not win such a conflict unless it was willing to put thousands of its troops on the ground, something its military brass refuses to do.

If attacked by Iran, what would happen? Israel would in all likelihood sustain high casualty numbers but would not face annihilation. No doubt an attack on Iran would trigger Shiite rage of tsunami proportions across the Fertile Crescent, including attacks from Hezbollah in Lebanon. To counter such attacks, the US has installed defensive Patriot Missiles in Israel, Saudi Arabia, Kuwait and the Arab Emirates. This is meant to defend these states against intermediate range (Shihab-3) ballistic missiles that Washington suspects Iran would launch in response to a US and/or Israeli attack.[139] Israel also has some two hundred nuclear missiles in its arsenal.

While Israel is supplied militarily by the US, Hezbollah receives its arms from Syria and Iran.

2. Israel has every right to defend itself to maximum capacity against every minor Hezbollah infraction. Israel has the right to defend itself. No one disputes this fact, but proportionality is the issue here. The question of whether Israel's use of force involved excessive harm to civilians and civilian infrastructure in relation to Israel's legitimate military aims arises from the scale of Israel's bombing campaign inside Lebanon.[140] Marvin Kalb, a Senior Fellow at the Shorenstein Center on the Press at Harvard's Kennedy School of Government, argues that any reports that suggest that

....

139 Street, Paul. "They Wouldn't Attack Iran, Would They?" *ZNet*, April 18, 2007.
    http://www.zmag.org/content/showarticle.cfm?ItemID=12610

140 Friel, Howard. "What's the Matter with Harvard?" *ZNet*, May 16, 2007.
    http://zcommunications.org/znet/viewArticle/15414

Israel's response was disproportionate is due to anti-Israel bias. However, the evidence disproves this. Lebanese civilian casualties were higher than Israeli civilian casualties by a ratio of twenty-five to one – clearly a disproportionate response to the capturing of two soldiers. Israel launched more than seventeen thousand attacks at more than eight thousand targets. The number of explosives targeted at Lebanon far exceeded the four thousand rockets launched by Hezbollah. The destruction of civilian infrastructure in Lebanon was vastly more extensive than that in Israel. Only Israel killed UN personnel. Both sides used anti-personnel weapons against civilian targets but only Israel's cluster ordinances produced hundreds of thousands of lethal munitions that are still killing civilians and only Israel used white phosphorus bombs.[141]

3. The war began because Hezbollah captured two Israeli soldiers. The capture was but a pretext to begin the military operations against Hezbollah that had been planned for some time. Abductions were a routine occurrence along the border. It was common practice not just for Hezbollah to abduct Israeli soldiers but for Israel to take innocent Lebanese. As a 1998 Amnesty International paper stated: "By Israel's own admission, Lebanese detainees are being held as 'bargaining chips.' They are not detained because of some actions but to be exchanged for Israeli soldiers missing in action or killed in Lebanon. Most have now spent ten years or more in secret and isolated detention."[142]

According to Alastair Crooke, former Middle East adviser to European Union High Representative Javier Solana, the abduction of the two Israeli soldiers and the killing of eight others on July 12 took the Hezbollah leadership by surprise and were successful only because Hezbollah units on the border had standing

....

141 Shalom, Steven. Interviewed by Anthony Dimaggio. "Perilous Power: The Middle East and US Foreign Policy." *ZNet*, June 5, 2007. http://www.zmag.org
142 Amnesty International. AI INDEX: MDE 15/54/98. June 26, 1998.

orders to exploit Israeli military weaknesses.[143] Israeli soldiers near the border that day apparently violated standing operational procedures, left their vehicles in sight of Hezbollah emplacements, and did so while out of contact with high-echelon commanders and while out of sight of covering fire. An article in the July 13 *Jerusalem Post* explains how this probably happened. The high alert status that the northern border had been under since the capture of the Israeli soldier in Gaza three weeks earlier had been lifted three days prior to the Hezbollah capture of the two Israeli soldiers.[144]

That an Army unit could wander so close to the border without being covered by fire and could leave itself open to a Hezbollah attack has led Israeli officers to question why the unit was acting outside the normal chain of command and under whose orders.[145]

Contrary to the misreported events on the Israeli-Lebanese border on July 12, the Israeli daily *Haaretz* confirmed that: "A force of tanks and armored personnel carriers was immediately sent into Lebanon in hot pursuit. It was during this pursuit at about 11:00 A.M. that a Merkava tank drove over a powerful bomb, containing an estimated two hundred to three hundred kilograms of explosives, about seventy meters north of the border fence. The tank was almost completely destroyed and all four crew members were killed instantly. Over the next several hours, Israeli soldiers waged a fierce fight against Hezbollah gunmen ... During the course of this battle, at about 3:00 P.M., another soldier was killed and two were lightly wounded."[146]

4. Hezbollah deliberately targeted civilians. Hezbollah fired over four thousand Katyusha rockets into northern Israel, killing

143 Crooke, Alastair and Mark Perry. "How Hezbollah Defeated Israel. Part One: Winning the Intelligence War." *Conflicts Forum.* http://conflictsforum.org/cf-publications/articles-series

144 Andromidas, Dean. "Cheney Unleashes the Dogs of War." *Executive Intelligence Review*, July 21, 2006.

145 Crooke, Alastair and Mark Perry.

146 Ibid.

thirty-nine civilians, eighteen of whom were Israeli Arabs. However, only eight hundred of the four thousand Katyushas hit built-up areas, suggesting that Hezbollah was not trying to hit the center of Haifa and kill as many civilians as possible, but rather to strike the oil refinery, the naval docks and other military installations around Haifa.[147]

Human Rights Watch makes a valid charge against Hezbollah – that it filled many of its rockets with ball bearings and was therefore intent on killing and injuring as many civilians as possible. The damage inflicted by the ball bearings is not in itself proof that Hezbollah was trying to kill Israeli civilians, any more than Israel's use of far more lethal cluster bombs is proof that it wanted to kill Lebanese civilians. Both were acting according to the gruesome realities of war. They wanted to inflict as much damage as possible with each rocket strike.[148]

The second criticism made by Human Rights Watch, which I suspect has more to do with appeasing its critics, is that because Hezbollah's rockets are rudimentary and lack sophisticated guidance systems they are as good as indiscriminate. According to Jonathan Cook, that conclusion is wrong both logically and semantically. The rockets are mostly not discriminate, though presumably some misfire, as do Israeli missiles, but rather the Katyushas are not precise.[149] Regardless, according to Human Rights Watch, this still makes Hezbollah's rocket attacks war crimes. This also means Israel's missile strikes and bombardments of Lebanon are war crimes on the same or greater scale.

5. Israel's air force tried to avoid harming Lebanese civilians by leafleting them before an attack to warn them that they must leave. Israel argues that only those who belonged to Hezbollah or gave it

....

147 Marcus, Yoel. "Oh, What a War." *Haaretz*, July 13, 2007.

148 Cook, Jonathan. "Hypocrisy and the Clamor Against Hezbollah." *CounterPunch*, August 9, 2006.

149 Ibid.

succor remained behind in South Lebanon and they were, therefore, legitimate targets. Hezbollah has done precisely the same. In speeches, Nasrallah repeatedly warned Israeli residents in Haifa, Afula, Hadera and Tel Aviv that Hezbollah will hit their cities with rockets days before it actually did so.

Beyond the futility of armed force, and ultimately more critical is the fact that war in our time inevitably results in the indiscriminate killing of large numbers of people. War, therefore, is terrorism. Wars waged by nations, whether the US or Israel, are a hundred times more deadly for innocent people than the attacks by Hamas or Hezbollah, vicious as they are.[150]

6. Israel was justified in dropping bombs where ordinary people lived because Hezbollah hid among the civilian population. Human Rights Watch could find no evidence to support Israel's claim that Hezbollah hid among civilians. Mitch Prothero, who covered the war from South Lebanon, concurred. "Throughout the thirty-four-day war, Israeli planes high above civilian areas made decisions on what to strike. They dropped huge bombs capable of killing things for hundreds of meters around their targets, and then blamed the inevitable civilian deaths on Hezbollah terrorists who callously used the civilian infrastructure for protection." According to Prothero, Hezbollah fighters avoided civilians. Much smarter and better trained than the PLO or Hamas, they know that if they mingle with civilians they will sooner or later be betrayed by collaborators.[151]

According to a July 2007 article in *Haaretz*, Israeli military sources now admit that most of the rockets fired against Israel during the 2006 war were launched from nature reserves and not from urban areas.[152]

....

150 Zinn, Howard. "War Is Not a Solution to Terrorism." *Boston Globe*, September 2, 2006.

151 Prothero, Mitch. "The 'Hiding Among Civilians' Myth." *Salon.com*, July 28, 2006. http://www.salon.com/news/feature/2006/07/28/hezbollah/index_np.html

152 Cook, Jonathan. "Revisiting the Summer War." *Electronic Lebanon*, August 16, 2007.

7. Israel's killing of civilians was accidental. As Israel sees it, the killing of innocent Lebanese is accidental, whereas the deaths caused by Hezbollah rockets are deliberate.[153] This is a false distinction. If a bomb is deliberately dropped on a house or a vehicle on the grounds that a suspected terrorist is inside, the resulting deaths of women and children may not be intentional. But neither are they accidental; rather, they are inevitable. So, if an action will inevitably kill innocent people, it is immoral, whether perpetrated by Israel or Hezbollah.[154]

In the south, where Shiites dominate, just about everyone supports Hezbollah. Does mere support for Hezbollah, or even participation in Hezbollah activities, mean your house and family are fair game? Do you need to fire rockets from your front yard? Or is it enough to be a political activist to be on the receiving end of an Israeli bomb?[155] The southern suburb of Beirut was repeatedly referred to as a Hezbollah stronghold as though using that distinction gave Israel the justification to bomb it into rubble. This so-called stronghold, home to some one hundred thousand refugees who fled Israeli aggression, did also house some offices of the political wing of Hezbollah. By choosing to treat the political members, the ones who supplied much of the humanitarian aid and the social protection for the poorest people as fighters is the same as targeting innocent civilians.

8. Hezbollah is a terrorist organization. The US, Israel, the Netherlands, Canada and the United Kingdom are the only countries that have classified Hezbollah as a terrorist organization. It is often associated with the bombing of the American Embassy in Beirut in 1983 and the Marine and French barracks in October of the same year. According to Augustus Richard Norton in his book *Hezbollah: A Short Story*, "There is little question that the attacks were carried out by Lebanese Shiite militants, under Iranian direc-

....

153 Zinn, Howard.
154 Ibid.
155 Prothero, Mitch.

tion." An investigating committee established by the American government described the barracks bombing as an "act of war" and found Iran largely responsible. Iran is also widely believed to be responsible for the earlier suicide bombing of the embassy.[156] Robert Baer, a former CIA agent with extensive experience in Lebanon was even more precise: "Hezbollah didn't do the US Embassy in 1983 or the Marines. It was the Iranians. It's a political issue in the US because the Israelis want the Americans to go after Hezbollah."[157]

Lebanon became infamous in the 1980s for the kidnapping of Westerners, thirty in all. The first four victims were, in fact, four Iranian diplomats snatched by the Lebanese Forces, a Maronite Christian militia, and subsequently murdered.[158] There was no "kidnapping-central" but a cabal of militants, some linked to Hezbollah, others in various other gangs and groups including some that were in the hostage business, selling and trading hostages for profit. According to Giandominico Picco, who played the lead role in many of the hostage negotiations, Syria had almost no influence over the kidnappers and Iran's leverage was operationally limited.[159] The hostage crisis gave rise to Iran-Contra, the 1986 scandal that revealed the willingness of then-US President Ronald Reagan to trade arms to Iran in return for the freeing of hostages. Unfortunately the hostage releases made possible by these deals was shortly followed by the snatching of others, and four more years would pass before the hostage era ended in Lebanon.[160]

"Terrorist" is a useful rhetorical bludgeon that Israel and the US have wielded to outlaw or de-humanize radical or revolutionary groups. The PLO was labeled for years as a terrorist group just as Hamas and Hezbollah are now.

························

156 Norton, Augustus Richard. *Hezbollah: A Short Story*. Princeton University Press, Princeton, 2007.
157 Ibid.
158 Ibid.
159 Ibid.
160 Ibid.

9. Hezbollah acted on orders from Syria and Iran. According to Anthony Cordesman of the Center for Strategic and International Studies, no serving Israeli official, intelligence officer or other military officer felt that Hezbollah acted under the direction of either Iran or Syria. This significant finding is based on information he gathered while in Israel. This directly contradicts Richard Haas, President of the Council on Foreign Relations, who claimed that Hezbollah would not have acted without the approval and direction of Iran. According to Cordesman, Iran and Syria did conduct a massive build-up of the Hezbollah's arms over a period of more than half a decade and that Iran's 747s routinely offloaded arms in Syrian airports. Syria provided trucks and shipped in arms and armed vehicles through the north and across the Bekaa.[161] According to Cordesman, "The issue of who was using whom, however, is answered by saying all sides – Hezbollah, Iran and Syria – were perfectly happy to use each other. Israel feels that Nasrallah initiated the abduction on his own, and that Iran and Syria were forced to support him once Israel massively escalated."

. . .

During and immediately following the 2006 war, the media, to its credit, focused a great deal of attention on the senseless bombing of power stations, the international airport, water treatment plants, telecommunication towers, industrial and food storage warehouses, grain silos, Liban Lait, the country's largest dairy farm, Maliban, the second largest glassworks factory in the Middle East, plastics and tissue paper factories, lumber mills and pharmaceutical plants – all non-strategic targets whose destruction appeared to be part of a concerted effort to weaken an already fragile Lebanese economy.

Scant attention has been paid, however, to Israel's deliberate bombing of one of Lebanon's greatest cultural treasures – its intellectual and scholarly life.

....

161 Cordesman, Anthony. "Preliminary Lessons of the Israeli-Hezbollah War." Center for Strategic and International Studies, October 17, 2006. www.csis.org

During the thirty-four days of bombardment, the Israeli Air Force targeted more than twenty publishing houses and research institutes in Beirut, including the warehouses of Dar al-Saqi, the popular London and Beirut based publisher of novels and literary nonfiction, and Dar al-Fikr al-Lubnani, a purveyor of educational guides and children's books. Israel also bombed the archives of *An-Nahar*, the Arab daily newspaper, the library of the prestigious Ecoles des Lettres, the publishing houses of Rissaia and Ibn Hazim and the laboratories of Lebanese University's Faculty of Science. Since Lebanon produces about seventy percent of the books distributed throughout the Middle East and beyond, these losses are profound. In 2006 at Book Expo America, my editor Ian Leask and I had the privilege of meeting with some of these publishers. It is not enough to say how outraged we are that such a vibrant part of Lebanon's diverse culture has been largely destroyed.

Dar al-Hadi, a publishing house located near Beirut's southern suburb, lost its entire stock of more than eight hundred titles. While it publishes books on religion and politics, it also publishes novels, books on nutrition, pedagogical resources and books on philosophy and the sciences and was about to add children's books. "We are not in any way affiliated with Hezbollah and get no funding from their organization," says its general manager, Abdel al-Amine. "Everyone knows that Hezbollah fighters are well read and educated. Some of them probably visited our bookstores at one time or another, but what was Israel thinking when it bombed our publishing houses? Did it think that by destroying books that it would weaken the resistance and destroy its ideology?"

10

DESPAIR OR HOPE?

Israel's paranoia and sense of insecurity, particularly with its still vivid memories of the Holocaust, is justified. Given the less than desirable outcome in its war with Hezbollah, the real or perceived threats from Syria and the possible future nuclear armament of Iran, it is also understandable from an Israeli point of view that the State of Israel would feel the need to attempt once again to re-define its military deterrence, to definitively crush Hezbollah and establish a permanent presence in South Lebanon.

The people of South Lebanon, for their part, feel incredibly bur-dened by the constant threat emanating from Israel on the other side of their border. They still reel from the injustices inflicted on them by Israel's twenty-two-year occupation when they saw their lives, their freedoms and basic human rights trampled on without so much as a yawn from the international community. In 2000, when the Israelis finally demanded that their troops come home, the Lebanese knew that it was not because of the immorality of brutally occupying two hundred thousand of their people. The protests, led mostly by women, focused exclusively on the blood of Israeli soldiers spilled in Lebanon in vain. Nothing would have been more important, of course, to an Israeli mother, sister or wife than their loved ones' lives, just as nothing is more important to a Lebanese mother, sister or wife from South Lebanon than the lives of their loved ones who steadfastly defend their villages.

The Israeli government casually talks of establishing a security zone in South Lebanon again as though no one lives there. Such talk by their leaders leads the average Israeli to believe that South Lebanon is a land of bloodthirsty Shiite terrorists, intent on destroying Israel, and so it is justifiable to ethnically cleanse the area to safeguard Israel's northern border. It is a modern-day version of Chaim Weizmann's "a land without people for a people without land" theme all over again.

In the months leading up to the war in Lebanon, the Hezbollah leadership, for its part, showed a total disregard for its constituents in South Lebanon. The country, for the first time since the end of the civil war, was preparing for a record summer tourist season. Hotels in the mountains and along the coast from Tyre to Sidon to Beirut and Byblos were booked solid for three months. It was next to impossible to buy a seat on any airline flying to Beirut. Lebanese officials were convinced the country had finally recovered from its image of civil strife. To guarantee success they obtained promises from every political party that they would do nothing to jeopardize the summer season. Hezbollah agreed, pledging publicly to behave.

This, despite the fact that tensions between them and Israel had been growing for months. In November 2005 Hezbollah, as it promised it would, tried to capture several soldiers, this time in Ghajar, a Lebanese village near the Golan Heights. In May 2006 in a typical tit for tat border exchange Hezbollah fired on an Israeli border post; Israel retaliated, shelling multiple Hezbollah positions along the Blue Line. What did all of this mean? Was Hezbollah trying to provoke a fight despite its promise to Lebanese government officials? I still find Nasrallah's admission that had he known Israel would retaliate with such force he would not have captured the two Israeli soldiers troubling, if not downright disingenuous. Did he stop to think that a provocation on his part would spell death and destruction for his people in South Lebanon? Did he care or did he assume that he could ride the wave of broad support he enjoyed, thus taking advantage of an already disenfranchised people for his own political gain? Post-war, the Lebanese people were, in fact, less angry with Hezbollah, in spite of the high death count and devastation, than at Israel for inflicting collective punishment on an entire population. Also, demands for Hezbollah to disarm its militia fell by the wayside, a development that surely did not go unnoticed by Nasrallah. Was that coincidental or was that his intention all along?

This war, in fact, produced few winners. Lebanon is a bitterly divided country. Israel fares no better with its hollow leadership itching for another war. The vast majority of Lebanese and Israelis are despaired of ever living normal lives again. These sad truths stated, how difficult would it really be to promote peace as an option to war and make it work?

This question prompted me to revisit something I wrote in my memoir *A Beirut Heart* about the real possibility of peace in the Middle East, if only the leaders would oblige. This particular scene takes place in 1976. Civil war is raging in Beirut and my family and I had just escaped on an apple boat to Syria. Upon landing in the seaport town of Lattakia, my husband Michel was unexpectedly arrested. During the interrogation his Syrian guards questioned him not about the supposed charges against him but about Israel. They wanted to know about Israeli technology and what kind of products they made, whether or not America supplied Israel with all its weapons or if the Israelis manufactured their own. Did Israel really have the best hospitals in the Middle East? The mother of one soldier needed open heart surgery. "How wonderful it would be," he said, "if one day we could get into our cars and drive to Israel for treatment."

Even after living the past twenty-three years in tranquil Eau Claire, Wisconsin, I still reflect on and appreciate how wonderful peace is, when allowed to happen. From time to time I think about dodging snipers and running into shelters, about my apron with its bullet hole, and about rescuing my children from school. I cannot go back to live in Beirut and risk my hard-won sanity, and I have finally accepted that. But I can write about the horrors of war so that our collective national memory can never say, "We didn't know." I can bring to light the voices of the ordinary people in Haifa, in Bint Jbeil, in Beirut, in Gaza and the West Bank who scream, "Stop these horrors. We want to live in peace."

Three teenage girls I interviewed at their Ramallah high school in the West Bank in March 2002 spoke most succinctly about their vision for peace and how it would work. To my question, "If you were in charge of the Palestinian Authority, what would you do to implement peace?" the girls responded:

I would forget about Jerusalem, boundaries, the right of return, and just be one nation. We are all brothers and sisters, all from one family. I am certain most Israeli children have the same feelings, the same imagination of life, as it can and should be. We will talk with them. They will understand that we can, that it is possible, to live together. Right now, young Israelis live healthy childhoods. They go to sports events, attend parties and play outdoors. All we do is wake up, go to school, return home, listen to machine gun fire and Apache gunships firing missiles and tanks rolling down our streets. We can't sleep. We have to get up early to go to school. Our grades are dropping because we cannot concentrate on our studies. This is our life now. We have been deprived of our childhoods and now we are teenagers. This is not a happy time for us. This is why we say, forget the leaders. All they want is war. They care nothing for our wants and needs.

And recall the words of the Israeli soldier I interviewed.

I am young and don't want to spend my whole life preparing for war. In Israel we have a war mentality. We never seem to talk about peace. It is as if saying the word is being disloyal to the State of Israel. I am ready to live in peace with my neighbors. I think Hezbollah would do the same. Why aren't our leaders willing to take the leap?

Sadly, from all indications, peace is not on the horizon.

The United States is recruiting a cadre of docile Arab rulers, willing to acquiesce to the West yet authoritarian enough to control their own people. The Bush administration calls this part of his plan for a new Middle East. The prominent members thus far include King Abdullah of Jordan, Egypt's Hosni Mubarak and King Abdullah of Saudi Arabia, none of whom want to see the regional power balance disturbed by a dominant Iran and its perceived lackey, Hezbollah. Lebanon's Fouad Siniora and the Palestinian Authority's Mahmoud Abbas have been invited to join this special club if they agree to play by the rules of the game. In the case of the latter two, they have been tasked with eliminating, or at the very least disarming, Hezbollah and Hamas. The al-Qaeda-linked insurgents already well entrenched in Lebanon, brought in as a counterbalance to Hezbollah, are likely the tool Siniora will use to carry out his assignment.[162]

On June 27, 2006, Hamas signed a document that effectively recognized the State of Israel, accepting a two-state solution for the creation of a sovereign Palestinian state side-by-side with Israel. Both Israel and the US ignored Hamas's declaration. In doing so they lost an unprecedented opportunity to politically engage a Hamas government that had the ability to control and influence the various radical militias, and convince them that peace was the only option.[163] To anyone interested in lasting peace, this recognition on the part of Hamas should have been welcome news. Since the message was ignored, is it not fair to ask if Israel really wants peace? If Israel does not seek peace, then is it not logical to argue that Israel is threatened only for reasons that are traceable back to its own disproportionate actions and for its unwillingness to choose peace over endless war? The captured Israeli soldiers are a case in point. Their plight is rarely mentioned in the media; even leaked reports on July 29, 2007 in the Israeli daily, *Haaretz*, suggesting that one of the soldiers being held in Lebanon may have died stirred little interest outside his family and circle of friends.

Israel can behave in any manner it chooses because it is given extraordinary immunity by the US in the form of political, diplomatic and strategic support, even to the point of receiving $300 million in aviation fuel during the July war so as to continue

· ·

162 Amiri, Rannie. "Nasrallah in the Crosshairs." *CounterPunch*, July 21/22, 2007. http://www.counterpunch.org/amiri07212007.html.

163 Lin, Sharat G. "Chronology of the Latest Crisis in the Middle East." *CounterPunch*, July 25, 2006. http://www.counterpunch.org/lin07252006.html

destroying Lebanon's infrastructure.[164] On July 29, 2007, the US pledged an additional $30.4 billion in military aid to Israel over the next ten years. This is in addition to the $3 billion Israel already receives annually. The US gave Israel free rein in Lebanon, hoping for a significant military victory, because it still is confronted with the probability of two highly disagreeable developments: a nuclear-armed Iran sometime in the future (according to the IAEA no such arms exist at the present time) and continued chaos in Iraq. It urgently needs to regain control in the wider Middle East.

This is where Lebanon comes into George Bush's plans for a new Middle East.

The US's interference in Lebanon's internal affairs has catapulted the country into chaos. Intent on diminishing the Shiite's powerful role in Lebanese politics, the White House is seeking ways to reconfigure the army and security services to more effectively serve American interests. Of the new recruits in the Interior Ministry-run police force, Shiites constitute less than ten percent.

The Siniora government, which has only a slim parliamentary majority and suffers from sinking public support, is seen as being simultaneously in open confrontation with Israel yet supported by the US. This is not useful for the Siniora government, particularly in light of a poll conducted by Telhamy-Zogby in late July 2007, which showed that eighty percent of respondents in Arab states closest to Washington saw Israel and the US as posing the greatest threat to their security.[165] The poll suggested only six percent of the region considered Iran a threat. The same poll shows Shiite Hezbollah's leader, Hassan Nasrallah, to be the most popular leader in the Middle East. In Lebanon, this regional rift sets Hezbollah against the US-backed Sunni government, a majority of the

....

164 Seale, Patrick. "Why is Israel Destroying Lebanon?" *Al-Hayat*, July 21, 2006.
     http://www.informationclearinghouse.info/article14191.htm

165 Chassay, Clancy. "Bush Policy Pushes Lebanon to the Brink of Civil War."
     CounterPunch, July 26, 2007. http://www.counterpunch.org/chassay07262007.
     html

Druze community and the remnants of the country's Christian far right – a recipe for disaster.[166]

In an increasingly dangerous climate, and with little regard for events on the ground in Lebanon, the Bush administration has consistently vetoed attempts by the Lebanese factions to form a desperately needed national unity government. In his policy speech on July 23, 2007, George Bush suggested this trend was set to continue, describing a struggle between extremists and moderates playing out in Lebanon, "where Hezbollah and Syria and Iran are trying to destabilize the popularly elected government."[167]

The majority of Lebanese are very disturbed by Bush's interference in their country, particularly since it was Washington during the 2006 war that encouraged Israel's assault on their country and then refused all calls for a cease-fire.

The more the daily horror in Iraq worsens, the more the Bush administration clings to the purported success of Lebanon, once its poster boy for its now redundant "democratization" campaign. By allowing the build-up of armed groups like Fatah al-Islam, and obstructing compromise in a vain effort to empower an unpopular government, the White House is pushing Lebanon down a dangerous path toward civil conflict, and ultimately disintegration, as it is doing in Iraq and the Palestinian Occupied Territories.[168]

What can the vast majority of Lebanese, Israelis and Palestinians who are tired of endless wars and outside interference do to save their respective countries? As is rapidly becoming apparent in America, the democracy every country is encouraged to emulate, where an increasingly powerful Executive wields power at the expense of the vast majority of its citizens, seemingly very little. Is this reason for despair or reason to act in order to reverse this course and create some hope for our future?

I strongly encourage the latter and further argue that at no time

....

166 Ibid.
167 Ibid.
168 Ibid.

in recent history has our collective engagement been more urgently needed. The power of the people, be they American, Israeli, Palestinian or Lebanese, has been hijacked by the executive branch of the US government, by the warmongering leaders in Israel, by the corrupt Palestinian lackeys and in Lebanon by the puppets of foreign powers, be they American or Iranian.

In the case of the Palestinians, how does a popular upswing of democratic thinking take place against a backdrop of Israeli occupation? How does one actually vote the ineffectual leaders out of office in Lebanon or Israel when outside powers are pulling the strings? In the United States how does the majority regain its voice and halt the erosion of our constitution before dangerous precedents, already enacted, are set in stone?

The answer, though simple, is one we have forgotten. We actively and vigorously participate in the process of government. We become informed on issues affecting our foreign policy and our standing in the world so as to better differentiate fact from fiction. We vote and hold our politicians accountable for their actions. As citizens of the international community, these are our obligations; no one is exempt.

We have everything to gain. Peace, after all, is the cornerstone of world stability and a viable future.

FROM ANCIENT TIMES
TO THE PRESENT

In post-civil war Beirut (1994), under Martyr's Square, Lebanese archeologists discover an 8,000 year old city.

4000 B.C. – Sidon, in what is today South Lebanon, is already a prosperous city renowned for its glass work and purple dye, a color used to mark royalty.

3000 B.C. – Lebanon first appears in recorded history as a group of independent coastal cities inhabited by Canaanites, a Semitic people the Greeks called Phoenicians. Tyre and Sidon are prominent maritime and trading centers; Byblos and Berytus (Beirut) are commercial and religious centers.

1436 B.C. – Phoenician city-states are incorporated into the Egyptian Empire.

1300 B.C. – The Egyptian Empire weakens. Beginning in the 12th century B.C., the city-states regain their independence but only for about three centuries.

875 B.C. – Assyrian rule deprives Phoenician city-states of their independence. Both Tyre and Byblos rebel repeatedly. In the middle of the 8th century, the Assyrian ruler Tiglath-Pileser finally subdues the rebels and exacts extreme retribution.

815 B.C. – Despite repeated Assyrian aggression on the home front, Tyrian traders founded Carthage in present-day Tunisia, bringing their city fame and flourishing maritime trade.

721 B.C. – Tyre rebels again, this time against Sargon II who besieges the city and brutally punishes the population.

687 B.C. – Sidon rebels again too. The current Assyrian ruler, Esarhaddon, tears down the city, beheads its king and deports its inhabitants.

685–636 B.C. – City-states fall under Babylonian rule. Tyre resists Nebuchadnezzar's attempts to capture the city for thirteen years until it finally capitulates and its citizens are enslaved.

553–530 B.C. – Cyrus the Great reigns over the Persian Empire.

490–449 B.C. – Sidon provides Persia with the ships and seamen it needs during the Greco-Persian War.

339 B.C. – When the Persian Emperor, Artaxerxes III, attacks, Sidonians resist by locking their city gates. More than 40,000 residents die when the Emperor sets fire to the city.

332 B.C. – Sidon is too weak to oppose Alexander the Great and his army. The city manages to arrange a truce. Initially, Tyrians make no attempt to resist Alexander the Great and his army. It is only when Alexander tries to offer a sacrifice to Melkart, the Tyrian god, that people rebel. Alexander besieges Tyre for six months; the city falls and the people are sold into slavery.

323 B.C. – Alexander the Great dies. His empire is divided among his Macedonian generals. The eastern Mediterranean falls to Seleucus I (Seleucus Dynasty) while Egypt goes to Ptolemy.

64 B.C. – Rome adds Lebanon to its Empire. The Phoenician city-states, the mountains and the Bekaa Valley are included in a region called Syria. Beryte (present-day Beirut) is the capital of the region with a famous university center and the Roman Empire's first law school.

395 A.D. – Christianity is proclaimed the sole official religion of the entire Roman Empire. Maroun, a Christian hermit, lives along the Syrian border in the Bekaa Valley. After his death in 395 A.D., his followers become known as the Maronites. Of the seventeen different religious sects in present-day Lebanon, the Maronites are the largest Christian sect.

611 – Islam is founded when Muhammad begins receiving the Quran from God.

632 – Muhammad dies. His successor, Caliph Abu Bakr, brings Islam to Lebanon.

661 – Islam splits into Shiism and Sunnism. The Umayyad Dynasty, with its capital in Damascus, Syria, rules what we know today as the Middle East.

750 – The Abbassid Dynasty succeeds the Umayyads.

986 – The Druze religion develops out of Ismaili Islam (Ismail was Abraham's first born-son by Hagar, his wife's Egyptian maid).

1054 – The great Christian schism occurs with the Church of Rome and Constantinople splitting. The Christians of Lebanon are now part of the Eastern Church of Antioch, coming under the authority of Constantinople.

1096–1291 – The Crusades begin. In all, there are eight crusades spanning two centuries.

1201 – Druze begin to settle in Lebanon.

1282 – The Mameluks succeed the Umayyads.

1300–1918 – The Ottoman Empire spans some six hundred years. In 1453 the Ottomans capture Constantinople and rename it Istanbul.

1516 – The Ottomans defeat Mameluks and capture Lebanese and Syrian territories but Mount Lebanon remains unconquered.

1585–1635 – Fakhr al-Din Maan, a Druze, fights for Lebanese independence, defeats the Turks and brings Lebanon, Syria and Palestine under his control.

1697 – Bachir Shihab succeeds Fakhr al-Din Maan.

1788–1840 – Bachir II breaks away from the Ottoman Empire but is quickly removed from power.

1840 – The Druze and Christian Maronites, both refuged in Mount Lebanon, start independence movements. To curtail this activity, Ottomans pit Druze against Christians.

1860 – The Druze massacre 12,000 Maronite Christians. Emir Abd el-Kader, an Algerian who fled to Damascus after being defeated by the French in Algeria in 1844, offers the Maronites refuge. Now an ally of France, Kader is asked to undertake this rescue mission because French troops cannot get to the Chouf in time to save the Christians.

1916 – The Sykes-Picot Agreement, a secret document forged by Britain and France, carves up the Ottoman Empire even before it falls apart in 1918. Britain takes control of Palestine and Iraq; France receives what is now Lebanon and Syria.

1920 – The League of Nations mandates to France the five provinces that will make up present-day Lebanon. They are: Beirut, Tripoli, Sidon, Tyre and Akkar (in the north).

1926 – Lebanon's constitution specifies balance of power between various religious groups but France designs it to guarantee the political dominance of its Christian allies.

1943 – Lebanon gains its independence from France.

1948 – Creation of the State of Israel. Granted their independence just five years apart, Israel and Lebanon's relationship is not a harmonious one.

1958 – First Lebanese civil war occurs when the Muslims rally to pan-Arab calls by Egyptian President Nasser. US President Eisenhower sends 15,000 American Marines to Beirut.

1964 – The Palestinian Liberation Organization (PLO) is formed.

1967 – The June Israeli-Arab war results in Israel's occupation of the Golan Heights, the West Bank, East Jerusalem, Gaza and the Sinai Peninsula.

1969 – The Cairo Agreement is signed between the PLO and the Lebanese government in which the latter accepts the legitimacy of the PLO's presence in Lebanon and its right to pursue the struggle against Israel from Lebanese territory. This document diminishes Lebanon's authority and lays the foundation for the civil war.

1970 – PLO guerrillas are driven out of Jordan because of their cross-border raids into Israel. Arafat and his PLO set up their headquarters in Beirut's refugee camps and begin cross-border raids into Israel from South Lebanon.

1973 – The Yom Kippur War. On October 6, Egypt and Syria attack Israel in the Golan and in the Sinai in an attempt to recover their occupied lands taken in 1967. Israel defeats both Arab armies in the twenty-day war.

1975 – The PLO becomes a state-within-a-state in Lebanon. At the same time, Muslim and Christian differences reach a boiling point. The Muslims are unhappy with the inequitable distribution of political power which favors the Christians. Mass protest rallies take place across the country.

1975 – After an early morning attempted assassination of Pierre Gemayel, founder of the Christian Phalange Party, a busload of Palestinians is attacked by Christian militia that same afternoon. These two incidents touch off the civil war. Palestinians join with Druze-Muslim forces to fight the Christian militias. Fighting quickly spreads across Beirut.

1976 – Civil war intensifies. Christians massacre Palestinians in Quarantina and Tel el-Za-atar; Palestinians massacre Christians in Damour. Syrian troops enter Lebanon at the request of the Christians who are about to be defeated by the Palestinian-Druze-Muslim forces. Since Syrian President Assad's modus operandi is divide-and-rule, thereby eliminating any one dominant power, and because he dislikes both the PLO and the Druze leadership, Assad is happy to accommodate the Christians. The US gives tacit approval of Syria's actions thereby allowing 30,000 troops to enter Lebanon.[169]

1978 – The Israeli Army invades South Lebanon after Palestinian gunmen attack a bus in northern Israel. Israel withdraws under pressure from the US, leaving in its place a proxy force, the South Lebanon Army. UN Forces (UNIFIL) are sent to patrol South Lebanon.

1982

June 4 – The Israeli Army, led by Ariel Sharon, invades Lebanon on June 4th to wipe out the PLO presence. The siege of Beirut lasts seventy days.

August – Arafat threatens to turn Beirut into a "2nd Stalingrad" to fight Israeli forces to the last man. Lebanese leaders petition

....

169 Harris, William. *Faces of Lebanon: Sects, Wars and Global Extension*. Markus Wiener, Princeton, 1977, pp. 261–262.

Arafat to finally agree to leave Beirut. Syria and Tunisia agree to host departing PLO fighters. Arafat sets up headquarters in Tunisia.

August 23 – Bachir Gemayel is elected President of Lebanon.

August 25 – The Multinational Force, composed of American, French and Italian troops, arrives in Beirut. Their mission is to oversee the PLO departure and guarantee the safety of the Palestinians left behind in the camps.

September 10 – Without any consultation from Washington, Secretary of Defense Caspar Weinberger orders the Marines out of Beirut and back aboard their ships.

September 14 – Bachir Gemayel is assassinated.

September 16–18 – The Christian militia massacre thousands of Palestinians in the Sabra-Chatilla refugee camps in Beirut.

September 29 – The Multinational Force returns to Beirut with the mandate to "provide an interposition force at agreed locations." The soldiers will not be allowed to engage in combat or carry loaded guns.

1983

April – The US Embassy in Beirut is destroyed by Iranian-backed Islamic Jihad suicide bombers. Some of these same fighters will go on to join Hezbollah when it is formally founded in 1985. Sixty-three die in the blast, seventeen of whom belong to the CIA's Middle East contingent.

May – Lebanon and Israel sign a declaration of intent to make peace. Israel pledges a phased withdrawal from all of Lebanon, based upon a simultaneous withdrawal by Syria. Free of foreign intervention, Lebanon can then pursue a formal peace with Israel. The proposed treaty has one major flaw: it fails to inform the Syrian president of the deal. Syria initiates an all-out battle in Beirut to punish the Gemayel government for their collusion with America and Israel. Documents released in 2007 indicate that, while Syria at the time was acting in its own best interest, it also did the Lebanese a huge favor. If a formal peace treaty had been signed with Israel in 1983, it would have given Israel a major voice in the security of South Lebanon.

September – Israeli troops withdraw from the Chouf Mountains. Their departure unleashes a vicious battle between Druze and Christian militia that quickly spreads to Beirut.

October – The US Marine barracks and the French military headquarters are razed by the same Islamic Jihad suicide bombers. The CIA knows from intercepts that Iran is planning to attack American targets yet Marines are still not allowed to carry loaded guns. More than 300 American and French servicemen die.

1984–1987 – Muslim militants begin kidnapping Westerners, including CIA station chief William Buckley, who dies after being tortured. The Archbishop of Canterbury's envoy, Terry Waite, disappears in West Beirut while seeking the release of US hostages.

1985 – Hezbollah is formally founded. Its agenda: destruction of the State of Israel and the Islamization of Lebanon.

1988 – Lebanese parliament fails to elect a new president after the six-year term of Amine Gemayel ends. Rival prime ministers take office in East and West Beirut. General Michel Aoun, a Maronite, is named acting prime minister in East Beirut; former Prime Minister, Salim al Hoss, a Sunni, in West Beirut.

1989

May – General Aoun declares war on the Syrian Army, which still has a considerable presence in Lebanon. Several thousand Lebanese die in battle. Aoun flees the presidential palace and takes refuge in the French Embassy before being flown to France.

September – Lebanese leaders agree on a charter of national reconciliation known as the Taif Agreement.

1990 – Lebanon's fifteen-year civil war ends with 150,000 dead.

1991

January – First Gulf War begins. Syria agrees to participate in US-led invasion. In exchange for its cooperation, the US turns a blind eye to Syrian titular control of Lebanon.[170]

November 17 – Terry Waite is released after 1,763 days in captivity. His first four years were spent in solitary confinement.

1992 – Rafic Hariri is named Lebanon's Prime Minister. He remains in this post until 1998 during which time Lebanon, and Beirut in particular, enjoys a period of relative calm and prosperity. A self-made billionaire and business tycoon, he donates millions of dollars of his own money to help Lebanon recover from the ravages of civil war. He and his business partners form Solidere, the joint-stock company that almost single-handedly transforms and revives central Beirut following the Lebanese civil war. While remembered for this stellar achievement, Lebanese also remember that Hariri's company, Solidere, confiscated the land in the city's center, compensating no one for their lost real estate.

1993 – Following the death of seven Israeli soldiers in South Lebanon, Israel launches Operation Accountability, during which the Israeli Defense Forces (IDF) launch the heaviest artillery and air attacks on targets in South Lebanon since 1982. During this operation, 118 Lebanese civilians are killed and 500 are wounded.

1996 – April – Israel launches Operation Grapes of Wrath. The assault lasts seventeen days. Over 300,000 Lebanese are forced to flee their homes in South Lebanon. Some refugees seek shelter in the UN compound in Qana. Israel, claiming Hezbollah fighters are inside the camp, fires missiles on the camp, killing 101 civilians.

....

170 Landis, Joshua. "US-Syrian Escalation over Lebanon." *SyriaComment.com*, October 14, 2002, p.3.

2000

— Rafic Hariri is once again named Lebanon's Prime Minister.

— After a twenty-two-year occupation, Israel withdraws from all of Lebanon, except the Shebaa Farms area. Its withdrawal is due in large part to the guerrilla war conducted against it by Hezbollah.

2003 – Second Gulf War begins.

2004

— Lebanese President Emile Lahoud's term is due to expire. Under pressure from Syria, his term is extended three more years. Lahoud is pro-Syrian and a bitter enemy of Rafic Hariri, who resigns as Prime Minister in protest.

— Hariri works with France and the US to force Syria's withdrawal from Lebanon. They succeed in getting UN Resolution 1559 passed, which calls on Lebanon to establish its sovereignty over all its land, for all foreign forces to withdraw and for all militias to disband.

2005

February 14 – Rafic Hariri is assassinated when explosives equivalent to 300 kg. of C4 detonate as his motorcade drives past the Saint George Hotel in Beirut.

March 19–May 7 – In an apparent attempt to destabilize Lebanon, bombs begin exploding in mainly Christian areas of the city. Syria is immediately blamed although there is no proof of its involvement.

April – Syrian troops withdraw from Lebanon.

May 7 – Michel Aoun returns to Lebanon, ending his fifteen-year exile in France.

May 29–June 19 – The election period in which Lebanon elects a new Parliament for the first time in thirty years. The Hezbollah bloc that includes Michel Aoun's party, the Free Patriotic Movement, wins fourteen out of 128 seats in Parliament and is given two cabinet posts.

June 2 – Anti-Syrian journalist Samir Qasir is killed in a car bomb blast outside his home on Abdel Wahab Street in Achrafieh, a Christian neighborhood.

June 21 – Former Communist Party leader George Hawi, a strong critic of Syria, is killed by a remote control bomb.

July 12 – Defense Minister Elias Murr is seriously wounded in an assassination attempt.

September 25 – A television news journalist for the Lebanese Broadcasting Corporation, May Chidiac, is seriously wounded by a car bomb.

December 12 – Anti-Syrian member of Parliament and journalist Gibran Tueni and three others are killed in a car bomb attack.

2006

June – The summer of 2006 is Lebanon's best since the civil war ended in 1990. Hotels from Tyre in the South to Tripoli in the north are full to capacity. Some 25,000 Lebanese Americans are in Lebanon visiting family and friends.

July 12 – Hezbollah kidnaps two Israeli soldiers. Israel responds and a devastating thirty-four-day war ensues, killing some 1,109 Lebanese, leaving 800,000 homeless and destroying much of Lebanon's infrastructure. Hezbollah retaliates by sending some 4000 Katyusha rockets into northern Israel, killing thirty-nine civilians. One hundred twenty-two Israeli soldiers die in combat.

November 11 – Hezbollah, which is closely aligned with Iran, demands the formation of a new unity government. When this demand is not met, it walks out of the Siniora government.

November 21 – Industry Minister Pierre Gemayel, son of former President Amine Gemayel and grandson of Pierre, the founder of the Phalange Party, is assassinated.

November 24 – Without consultation with President Lahoud and without the participation of the Hezbollah bloc, which walked out of the government on November 11, Prime Minister Fouad Siniora calls on the UN to begin a probe into the Hariri assassination.

December 1 – When Hezbollah and its coalition partner, Michel Aoun, call for mass demonstrations, hundreds of thousands of people descend on the city's center. They vow to stay there until the Siniora government steps down.

December 6 – Release of the Baker-Hamilton Iraq Study Group report which, among other things, recommends that the Bush administration enter into talks with Syria and Iran in an effort to calm the region.

December 9 – Lebanese President Emile Lahoud refuses to endorse Siniora's decision to refer the UN report on Hariri's murder to an international tribunal since the government no longer meets the requirements of the country's power-sharing constitution. Siniora disagrees claiming he still has enough Cabinet members to achieve a quorum to approve the tribunal.

2007

January 13 – Anti-government demonstrations continue in the city center. Speaker of the House Nabih Berri and President Emile Lahoud continue to refuse to call for an extraordinary session of Parliament to vote on a UN probe into Hariri's death.

January 20 – The US State Department releases a report asserting that Israel violated the Arms Export Control Act when it blanketed South Lebanon with American-made cluster munitions during the 2006 war. International demining groups estimate that some 2.6 to 4 million submunitions were fired into Lebanon during the five-week war.

January 25 – A riot breaks out between Sunni and Shiite students at Beirut Arab University. Two students are killed and scores of protesters are wounded. Two days later, clashes erupt between government opponents and supporters. Cars are set on fire; tires strewn across major intersections are burned, causing major traffic jams while thugs roam the streets with clubs and chains.

February 2 – Prime Minister Siniora bypasses Berri and Lahoud and asks the UN Security Council to pass a resolution under Chapter 7 of the UN Charter to begin a probe. Such a court created under Chapter 7 relieves the Siniora government of the need to go to Parliament to vote on the tribunal.

February 6 – The UN signs the draft for a tribunal to try suspects in the Hariri killing. The draft will be returned to Lebanon for ratification in Parliament.

February 24 – The Lebanese and Israeli armies are in a state of alert on both sides of the barbed-wire fence separating the two countries. Lebanese soldiers on patrol in the border area of Kfar Kila were surprised when they found an Israeli patrol on its side of the border pointing guns at them. After the standoff, the Israeli troops agreed to pull back to the Israeli settlement of Metulla, a few hundred meters from the border. This is the third such incident in a month between the two armies.

February 27 – Lebanese police confiscate a batch of liquid explosives near the Ain el-Hilweh Palestinian camp near Sidon.

March 2 – Western intelligence agencies are concerned about the growing concentration of terror operatives in Lebanon who are associated with groups that derive their inspiration from al-Qaeda. According to intelligence reports, hundreds of Sunni terrorists from various Arab countries are currently living near Tyre and Sidon.

March 4 – Lebanese authorities seize a carload of automatic machine guns belonging to the Syrian Social Nationalist Party. This small Lebanese party, anti-Syrian in nature and therefore banned in Syria, is part of the Hezbollah bloc. One of its members allegedly assassinated Bachir Gemayel in September 1982.

March 22 – Israel has officially named the thirty-four-day war with Hezbollah the Second Lebanon War. According to the *Jerusalem Post*, Israel only gives names to those wars it wins.

March 31 – One hundred thirty-one days into the current standoff between the Hezbollah bloc and the Siniora government, the Lebanese are fed up with their politicians who arrived at an Arab Summit in Saudi Arabia, which was organized to help end the stalemate, in two delegations. Arab leaders essentially told the Lebanese officials to stop acting like children and resolve their differences. The worst affront to the Lebanese, particularly those in the south, is the current feuding about who will deliver the much needed aid to the south, which is still in need of billions of dollars to rebuild and return some 300,000 internally displaced people to their homes.

April 11 – Hezbollah leaders accuse the US administration of arming anti-Hezbollah militias and of seeking to undermine the Lebanese Army in moves which could plunge the country back into civil war. According to Hezbollah's deputy secretary general in an interview to *The Guardian*, "Dick Cheney has given orders for a covert war against Hezbollah." The accusation follows reports in the US and British media that the CIA has been authorized to take covert action again Hezbollah.

April 23 – An editorial by Orit Shobat in the Israeli daily *Haaretz* addresses the possibility of a sizable war in the summer of 2007. A "sizable war" is a code name for a war that includes Syria.

April 27 – Ziad Qabalan, a twenty-five-year-old man, and Ziad Ghandour, a twelve-year-old boy, are abducted and brutally murdered. Their bodies are found in the Chouf Mountains. It is rumored that Qabalan, a Sunni, was abducted in response to the killing of the Shiite during the clashes at Beirut Arab University in January.

May 1 – The Winograd Commission, an Israeli government board of inquiry set up in September 2006 to examine the preparation and conduct of both the government and military during the Second Lebanon War, releases its interim findings. The commission determines there were major failings in the decision-making process to go to war and in the way it was carried out. Prime Minister Olmert is heavily criticized in the report but he refuses to resign.

May 5 – A judicial source tells *The Daily Star*, a Lebanese newspaper, that the five brothers of Adnan Shamas, the Hezbollah supporter who was killed during the clashes on January 25 at Beirut Arab University, are suspects in the April 27 murder of Qabalan and Ghandour. Apparently Qabalan is the one who killed Shamas; the father of Ghandour is a well-known supporter of Walid Jumblatt, the Druze leader and a rival political foe of Hezbollah.

May 6 – Edmond Saab, editor-in chief of *An-Nahar*, a Beirut daily, calls for a state inquiry into Hezbollah's accountability for the war and for the devastation it has caused in Lebanon. "Had we launched our own mini-Winograd committee, it would have served to resolve the prolonged and protracted political stalemate that we now witness between the March 14th coalition and the Hezbollah bloc."

May 6 – Hezbollah rejects a UN tribunal to probe the Hariri killing.

May 6 – Michel Aoun says Lebanon's Christians will be in shock if he is not elected as the next president. He claims to have the support of seventy percent of all Christians in Lebanon and vows not to back off from nominating himself.

May 9 – UN Secretary-General Ban Ki-Moon places disarmament of Hezbollah, respect for the sovereignty and territorial integrity of Lebanon and the holding of free and fair presidential elections as the key challenges facing the Lebanese government.

May 11 – The *Rheinische Post*, a German daily, says that Israeli forces have been involved in three incidents with UN naval peacekeepers under German command off Lebanon's coast. In one incident several Israeli fighter jets made an approach toward a German frigate. Earlier, on April 30, the same frigate signaled that it was ready for combat when an Israeli speedboat approached the vessel traveling at around thirty knots without initially identifying itself.

May 11 – Siniora calls on Israel to adopt the Arab Peace Initiative. He says that military action does not give the people of Israel security. The condemnation by the Winograd committee should, he says, be an impetus for Israel to seek comprehensive peace with its neighbors.

May 20 – Presidential elections are due to take place no later than

September 25, 2007. Hezbollah warns that it will not recognize a president elected by a simple majority of Parliament and it lambastes those who desire a president appointed by the US.

May 20 – Members of a pro-al-Qaeda group called Fatah al-Islam infiltrate a refugee camp in Tripoli in northern Lebanon. A battle ensues when the insurgents attack Lebanese soldiers posted outside the camp. To date at least forty people have died, twenty-three of them soldiers. Siniora accuses Syria of sending the insurgents to destabilize the country.

May 20–21 – Two bombs explode, one in East Beirut, the other in West Beirut. Three people are killed.

May 21 – The Bush administration changes its position regarding a possible receptive Israeli response to Syrian President Bashar Assad's call for peace talks. The American change of heart is accompanied by several preconditions. Washington says Israel is entitled to discuss the future of the Golan Heights, security arrangements and peace with Syria. But Israel should not agree to any negotiations regarding Lebanon's future.[171]

May 22 – In an interview on CNN International's *Your World Today*,[172] Seymour Hersh says that the current battle between the Lebanese Army and Fatah al-Islam in the Palestinian camp in northern Lebanon is the unintended consequence of a plot devised by Dick Cheney, Elliott Abrams and Prince Bandar bin Sultan to covertly fund Sunni insurgents as a counterbalance to Hezbollah.

May 23 – A bomb explodes in the mountain resort of Aley, a Druze village east of Beirut, wounding fifteen people.

May 24 – Fighting rages between the Lebanese Army and Fatah al-Islam, a group of some 400 insurgents from Saudi Arabia,

....

171 Schiff, Ze'ev. "US About Face Gives Israel Green Light for Syria Dialogue." *Haaretz*, May 5, 2007.

172 Hersh, Seymour. "Bush Administration Arranged Support for Militants Attacking Lebanon." *Raw Story*, May 22, 2007, filed by David Edwards and Muriel Kane. www.rawstory.com

Pakistan, Algeria, Iraq and Tunisia. Apparently they slipped into the Nahr al-Bared camp in October 2006.[173]

May 24 – Lebanese journalist Michael Young claims Syria is responsible for Fatah al-Islam's presence in Lebanon. Syria, according to Young, wants to undermine the UN proposed tribunal and wants a decisive say in who becomes Lebanon's next president. The Assad regime never reconciled itself with its forced withdrawal from Lebanon and is now actively seeking to re-impose its hegemony over its neighbor through a network of allies and agents.[174]

May 25 –The humanitarian situation inside the Nahr al-Bared camp is rapidly deteriorating. Approximately 15,000 residents are still inside the camp; the rest have fled to a nearby Palestinian camp.

May 30 – A study done by the Global Peace Index says Lebanon is one of the least peaceful countries in the world. Out of 121 countries surveyed, Norway ranked the safest, Lebanon ranked 114th, Israel 119th and Iraq dead last.

June 1 – According to documents released by the National Archives in London, Shin Bet, Israel's Security Agency, played a major role in the hijacking of an Air France plane in 1976 by Palestinian terrorists in which twenty-four people were killed. "The hijack was the work of the PFLP (Popular Front for the Liberation of Palestine), a splinter group opposed to Arafat's PLO, and the Israeli Shin Bet. The operation was designed to torpedo the PLO's standing in France and to prevent what Israel saw as a growing rapprochement between the PLO and the Americans. Israel's nightmare was that it would see the imposition of a Pax Americana which would favor the PLO."[175]

June 3 – As fighting continues in the Nahr al-Bared camp, heavy

....

173 Lamb, Franklin. "Inside Nahr al-Bared and Bedawi Refugee Camps: Who's Behind the Fighting in North Lebanon?" *CounterPunch*. May 24, 2007 www.counterpunch.org/lamb05242007.html

174 Young, Michael. "Destruction and Deceit in North Lebanon." *The Daily Star*, May 24, 2007.

175 "Shin Bet Involved in 1976 Hijacking." *Jerusalem Post*, June 1, 2007.

clashes erupt in Sidon between the army and another Sunni extremist group.

June 11 – The Lebanese Center of Research and Studies warns that economic instability and security threats are driving many young, educated Lebanese abroad, creating a brain drain that threatens the country's future.

June 13 – Walid Eido, member of Parliament and of Saad Hariri's Future Movement Party, is assassinated in a massive car bomb. Eight others die also including Eido's oldest son, two bodyguards and several bystanders.

June 15 – The US State Department urges Americans to defer travel to Lebanon because of the ongoing violence.

June 16 – By-elections are scheduled for August 5 to replace two assassinated MPs, Walid Eido and Pierre Gemayel.

June 24 – Six members of the UNIFIL peacekeeping force are killed in a road side bomb attack in South Lebanon near Khiam. Pro-al-Qaeda insurgents are blamed for the bombing that killed three Spaniard and three Colombian soldiers.

June 29 – Hezbollah admits it is rearming. According to Timur Goksel, it is only a matter of time before war between Hezbollah and Israel breaks out again.

June 30 – A new Pew Research Center Global Attitudes Survey from 47 countries reveals that public attitudes toward the US continue to deteriorate. The American-Israeli push for war in Iraq and the continued pressure on Iran, Syria, Hamas and Hezbollah have sparked a new level of collective political resistance throughout the Middle East.

July 9 – Fighting continues in the Nahr al-Bared camp. Lebanese authorities identify the bodies of ten Saudis among the Fatah al-Islam insurgents.

July 11 – The UN's mapping experts determine that the controversial Shebaa Farms is Lebanese territory. The UN suggests Israel withdraw from the area as soon as possible. Foreign Minister Tzipi Livni and Prime Minister Olmert oppose the idea, saying there is no such thing as transferring a territory without a bilateral agreement.

July 12 – Benjamin Netanyahu blames Olmert for the failure to vanquish Hezbollah in the thirty-four-day Second Lebanon War, saying the biggest lesson we must learn from the war is that "weakness breeds attacks, strength repels them."

July 12 – French President Nicholas Sarkozy invites all Lebanese leaders caught up in the stand-off to Paris to try to help them settle their differences. Sarkozy's efforts will ultimately fail.

July 13 – Abdel-Mohsen al-Husseini, the mayor of Tyre, chides the Lebanese government for its continued neglect of the people in the south one year after the end of the war. One of the few officials who stayed in the south during the war, he opened his city to 40,000 displaced people. During the war, Tyre itself was an oasis of security. Husseini had an agreement with Hezbollah that no armed man would enter the city, thereby sparing it an Israeli assault.

To date, ninety percent of the people whose homes were destroyed by Israeli bombs have not received compensation to rebuild. Husseini says that the government also owes his city billions of dollars and that he does not have enough money to pay salaries anymore.

July 13 – The Syrian government tells UN envoy Michael Williams that it is willing to make peace with Israel and in the context of such an agreement is prepared to break its ties with Iran and Hezbollah.

July 16 – The Paris-hosted Lebanese dialogue to end the nine-month-old stalemate fails to adopt any of the French proposals on key issues. The Hezbollah block insists that a national unity with veto power be agreed to first before the adoption of any formula for presidential elections. Prior to the talks French officials held consultations with Iran. It was their hope that Iran would sway Hezbollah delegates into accepting certain key proposals that would have moved the talks forward.

July 16 – A roadside bomb targets a UNIFIL patrol near Tyre. Both Hezbollah and its Shiite counterpart, Amal, condemn the attack.

July 17 – Banking institutions predict that the Lebanese budget deficit will dramatically rise this year. Lebanon's external debt is also expected to rise over the next two years to $30.8 billion. This is equivalent to 124 percent of GDP or 187 percent of exports of goods and services.

July 18 – The UN bows to Israeli pressure and decides against releasing the report that confirms that the Shebaa Farms belongs to Lebanon. Israel claims releasing the report will reignite the conflict and give Hezbollah an excuse to renew hostilities.

July 19 – The French government, in its eagerness to restore stability in Lebanon, is learning that it must also accommodate the demands of both Syria and Iran, each of whom has a vested interest in bringing forth a new government that strengthens their hold over the Lebanese government.

July 19 – The US insists there is clear evidence of arms smuggling across the Syrian border to "terrorist groups" in Lebanon and accuses Tehran and Damascus of playing a negative role in Lebanon.

July 20 – The US House of Representatives introduces a resolution expressing support for the Lebanese government while condemning Syria and Iran for their ongoing roles in providing arms to Lebanese militias, particularly Hezbollah and Palestinian factions.

July 20 – The Israeli Knesset passes the Jewish National Fund Law which discriminates against its Arab citizens in who can and cannot own land in Israel. A clause in the bill states that "the leasing of Jewish National Fund lands for the purpose of settling Jews is not seen as unacceptable discrimination."

July 22 – Iran's President Mahmoud Ahmadinejad pledges to help Syria conduct nuclear research and provide it with $1 billion in military aid to purchase arms from Russia and North Korea.

A report in *Haaretz* claims there is disagreement between Syria and Iran over Lebanon and that Iran is trying to pressure Syria against conducting talks with Israel, in return for a favorable policy in Lebanon. This suggests that calls for peace by Bashar Assad have been made contrary to Iran's will and therefore greater importance should be attributed to them.

July 22 – Lebanese troops intensify their shelling of Fatah al-Islam militants inside Nahr al-Bared. The deployment inside the remains of the camp is slow because of demining operations and booby-traps set by the insurgents. Almost all of the estimated 30,000 residents have been successfully evacuated. The Lebanese Army has lost 128 soldiers to date while some 200 civilians have been killed.

July 24 – The Lebanese Army Commander, General Michel Suleiman, warns that he will resign if two competing governments emerge as a result of a presidential vacancy. Suleiman says he will not tolerate a political divide that will threaten Lebanon's unity and its military institution.

July 29 – German diplomatic sources say that one of the two Israeli soldiers captured by Hezbollah on July 12, 2006 is alive. This has not been confirmed by either Israel or Hezbollah.

July 29 – US pledges Israel an additional $30.4 billion in military aid over the next ten years. This is in addition to the $3.4 billion it already receives in military aid annually. The US proposes to sell, not give, Saudi Arabia advanced weaponry such as satellite-guided bombs, upgrades to its fighter jets and new naval vessels. This will come with a price tag of some $20 billion. Israel opposes the sale and urges the US Congress to vote against it.

July 29 – Aluf Benn, journalist from *Haaretz*, suggests the arms deal with Saudi Arabia and the expanded military aid to Israel can be understood in two ways. The former involves American domestic politics while the latter helps realign the balance of power in the Middle East at a time when Russia is supplying arms to Iran and Syria.

July 31 – President Bush calls for an international peace conference. Syria responds to this initiative by agreeing to take part: "Syria will support and participate in any international conference for peace."

July 31 – Clashes erupt between supporters of Amine Gemayel, who is running in the parliamentary bi-elections to choose a successor to his son who was assassinated in November 2006, and supporters of Michel Aoun's two candidates. The Maronite Patriarch, Nasrallah Sfeir, favors Amine Gemayel's candidacy, urging the warring sides to adhere to tradition and unite in times of crisis. According to Lebanese electoral tradition, when a parliamentary seat is vacated by assassination that seat is given to a family member.

August 1 – Israel allows the transfer of 1,000 rifles from Jordan to the security forces loyal to PA President Abbas.

August 2 – President Bush declares a "national emergency to deal with the threats in Lebanon" which aim to undermine the Siniora government and reassert Syrian control.

August 7 – Even though Amine Gemayel loses the Metn election to Michel Aoun's candidate, Camille Khoury, by a narrow margin, he claims he is still the true representative of the Christians and stressed that the forthcoming head of state should be chosen from the March 14th alliance.

August 7 – The US keeps a vigil on Lebanese businessmen and other wealthy American residents donating money to General Michel Aoun and his Free Patriot Movement. The new Bush order will block the property and interests of persons determined by the Secretary of Treasury and the Secretary of State to have taken or to pose a significant risk of taking actions including acts of violence that have the purpose or effect of undermining Lebanon's democratic processes or institutions or contributing to the breakdown of the rule of law in Lebanon.

August 9 – Lebanon continues to deal with the devastating ecological disaster wreaked on it by Israeli air strikes during the 2006 war. Vast areas of the Lebanese coast are still severely polluted. Although thousands of tons of oil and other debris have been removed, large quantities of waste are still on site endangering the ecosystem while awaiting disposal.

In a behind-the-scene plot coordinated with the Siniora

government, the US State Department removes Lebanon's Ambassador to the US, Farid Abboud, an ally of Lebanese President Emile Lahoud, and replaces him with career diplomat, Antoine Chedid. Even though Lebanese President Lahoud, a Syrian ally, refused to sign Chedid's letter of recommendation, Secretary Rice welcomed Chedid to his post, thereby officially recognizing him as Lebanon's new ambassador to the US.

August 10 – President Bush announces that "Washington cannot live" with Tehran's support for Hezbollah.

August 23 – The March 14th Alliance will elect a new president by simple majority and rejects the principle of choosing a head of state by consensus as proposed by the Hezbollah bloc.

August 31 – Speaker of Parliament Nabih Berri remains committed to holding presidential elections on time. "Only an earthquake" will prevent him from calling for an electoral session on September 25, 2007.

He also announces that the Hezbollah-led opposition is ready to give up its demand for the formation of a new government with veto powers in return for consensus on the new president.

Meanwhile, President Lahoud announces he will name General Michel Suleiman, Lebanon's Army Commander, his provisional successor if the warring political factions fail to agree on a new head of state.

September 3 – After 105 days of intense fighting, the Lebanese Army declares victory over Fatah al-Islam but at a price. One hundred sixty-three of its soldiers die in battle.

September 5 – Berri officially calls for a special session on September 25 to elect a new president.

September 6 – Israel invades Syrian airspace and bombs what it claims was a convoy of weapons shipments destined for Hezbollah. Other Israeli reports suggest the site was being used to manufacture nuclear weapons.

September 9 – One hundred twenty-eight deputies have from September 25 to November 24 to elect a president who, in accordance with tradition, is drawn from the country's Christian Maronite community.

September 12 – Israel claims that North Korea is supplying Syria with nuclear material.

September 13 – The March 14th Alliance urges all parties to enter into negotiations to elect a new president. "Let's not say we want elections on the basis of a half-plus-one vote and let the opposition not block elections under the pretext of a two-third quorum." Berri reiterates that the opposition is willing to drop its demand for a national unity government on condition the country's feuding political factions agree on a consensus presidential candidate.

September 14 – Maronite Patriarch Nasrallah Sfeir voices disappointment over foreign meddling in Lebanon. "Foreign interference in Lebanon's internal issues is the worst thing happening to Lebanon."

September 15 – US Ambassador to Lebanon Jeffrey Feltman says his country will not recognize anyone it views as a renegade head of state; that includes anyone named by outgoing President Emile Lahoud as interim president.

September 25 – Berri adjourns the crucial parliamentary session to elect a new president until October 23.

September 27 – US House votes to back the Siniora government by a vote of 415 to 2. Congressman Gary Ackerman, chairman of the House Subcommittee on the Middle East and South Asia, warned the House that "Lebanon's being bullied by Iran, Syria and their proxies, Hezbollah, Amal and Michel Aoun's Free Patriotic Movement." He accused Damascus and Tehran of destabilizing Lebanon in order to pursue their national interests.

October 16 – Hezbollah and Israel exchange the remains of an Israeli civilian for a captive Lebanese fighter and the bodies of two of his comrades.

October 18 – Israel still refuses to provide Lebanon with maps of where it dropped cluster bombs.

Army Commander General Michel Suleiman denies news reports that the US wants to establish an advance military base for its forces in Lebanon.

October 19 – Syria accuses the US of interfering in Lebanon's affairs.

October 20 – Israel rejects a recommendation by the UN to begin negotiations with Lebanon over the disputed Shebaa Farms area.

A senior Pentagon official tells Lebanese television that the US military wants to build a strategic partnership with Lebanon's army. A stronger Lebanese Army would reduce the need for resistance movements to keep weapons to defend themselves.

October 21 – Berri chooses November 6 as the chosen date to convene Parliament to elect a new president.

US Vice President Dick Cheney says the US will not permit Iran to get nuclear weapons. He accuses Syria of trying to undermine free presidential elections in Lebanon.

October 22 – Hezbollah threatens to treat US troops as a hostile occupying force should the US decide to set up a military base in Lebanon.

Presidential elections are postponed until November 12.

October 25 – Israeli Foreign Minister Tzipi Livni says that Iranian nuclear weapons, if they exist, do not pose an existential threat to Israel. She criticizes Prime Minister Ehud Olmert for making an issue of the Iranian bomb and claims that he is attempting to rally the public around him by playing on people's most basic fears.

October 29 – The US denies allegations about its intention to set up military bases in Lebanon.

October 31 – According to Israel, Hezbollah has tripled its arsenal of C-802 land-to-sea missiles and has rehabilitated its military strength north of the Litani River.

November 1 – Lebanon accuses Israel of nearly 300 encroachments into Lebanese air space since the end of the Israeli-Hezbollah War.

November 2 – UN cartographers define the Shebaa Farms area and determine that it belongs to Lebanon. Since Israel disputes this claim both Lebanon and Syria have asked the UN to assume custodial responsibility for the area until it can formally be returned to Lebanon.

The Lebanese Army fires on Israeli warplanes as it violates South Lebanon's airspace.

November 3 – US Secretary of State Rice warns against any diplomatic moves to resolve the standoff between Lebanon's rival political camps through compromise. Her comments come as Lebanon's rival camps try to reach a deal over a successor to President Lahoud who must step down on November 24.

November 23 – Lebanese politicians fail for the 7th time to elect a new president.

November 30 – US Ambassador Jeffrey Feltman says Lebanese MPs should consider amending the Lebanese constitution to allow the election of Army Commander General Michel Suleiman, a possible consensus candidate.

December 2 – Serious efforts are underway to achieve consensus on General Suleiman to serve as Lebanon's next president. March 14th Alliance supports Suleiman but it is unclear at this time if Michel Aoun and Hezbollah support him.

December 4 – According to a National Intelligence Report, Iran halted its nuclear weapons development program in the fall of 2003. Director of National Intelligence Mike McConnell says an exception was made to release this important information because the latest assessment by the Bush administration on Iran's nuclear program had been very influential in public debate about the US policy toward Iran. The IAEA says the report is consistent with its own findings.

December 5 – Israel's assessment of Iran's nuclear program differs from the recently released US Intelligence Report and insists that Iran continues to produce uranium.

Palestinian President Mahmoud Abbas agrees to Israel's pre-conditions for negotiations. He dissolves the Palestinian government of national unity; he closes down more than one hundred Hamas-affiliated charities and sends his Palestinian security forces into Nablus to liquidate the resistance cells that have held out against the Israeli army for the last seven years. In return for his cooperation, he learns of Olmert's plan to enlarge the Israeli settlement of Har Homa near Bethlehem by 300 homes, that the E-I corridor linking Jerusalem to Ma-aleh Adumin settlement in the West Bank with 3,500 new homes is underway and that a military assault on Gaza is imminent.

December 5 – Both political camps in Lebanon agree to endorse the candidacy of General Michel Suleiman, Commander of the Lebanese Armed Forces. However, they disagree on how to amend the constitution which bars a senior public servant from running.

December 6 – Michel Aoun insists that the new president have veto power, something that was taken away from the Christian president in the Taif Agreement. Aoun also argues for an agreement on the formation of the forthcoming cabinet prior to presidential elections.

December 7 – Again, Lebanon postpones presidential elections.

Lebanon's acting Foreign Minister blames Beirut's political paralysis on outside powers using the country as a proxy battleground.

US Defense Secretary Robert Gates blames Iran, not Israel, for Lebanon's instability.

Iran says it supports any solution the various Lebanese factions agree on to settle the ongoing political crisis.

December 11 – The Lebanese media predicts a new president will not be elected before the end of the year or even by March '08 because of the continued standoff between the Siniora government and the Hezbollah bloc.

December 12 – Brigadier General Francois el-Hajj is assassinated by a car bomb. He was considered a leading candidate to succeed the head of the military if General Michel Suleiman is elected Lebanon's next president.

December 16 – US Special Envoy David Welch orders the Siniora government to elect a new president immediately.

December 17 – The Bush administration attempts to coerce the U.N. to endorse the Siniora government. The Bush plan is to push the Lebanese Army, which has always tried to maintain a neutral stance, to join forces with UNIFIL against Hezbollah. According to Franklin Lamb, Lebanon's best hope for national consensus is cooperation between the Lebanese Army, Hezbollah and UNIFIL. This tripartite cooperation could enable Lebanon to secure and safeguard its southern border and airspace and help rebuild the country.

December 22 – Israel rejects Hamas's truce offer and steps up its attacks on Gaza.

December 24 – The Israeli army, after a year-long probe, announces that its use of cluster bombs across South Lebanon was a concrete military necessity and did not violate international humanitarian law.

December 24 – The Siniora government, which legally should have dissolved when President Lahoud stepped down as president, decided to amend the constitution to facilitate the election of Michel Suleiman. They did this without calling parliament into session, knowing full well that the opposition would cry foul.

. . .

As this book goes to print, Lebanon's leaders, after twelve attempts, have failed to elect a new president. Meanwhile, David Welch and Elliott Abrams are pushing the March 14 coalition into a confrontation with the Hezbollah bloc. This is a dangerous move on the part of the Bush administration because while the opposition will most likely resist, tensions will rise between Sunnis and Shiites nonetheless.

CAST OF CHARACTERS, PLACES AND EVENTS

Elliott Abrams – Currently, he holds the post of Deputy National Security Advisor on Middle East Affairs.

As Ronald Reagan's Assistant Secretary of State for Human Rights and Humanitarian Affairs in the 1980s, he oversaw US foreign policy in Latin America. He actively covered up some of the worst atrocities committed by the US-sponsored Contras. During a *Nightline* appearance in 1985, he was asked about reports that the US-funded Salvadorian military had slaughtered civilians. Abrams maintained that no such massacres occurred. Yet, at the 1993 UN truth-commission which examined 22,000 atrocities that occurred during the twelve-year civil war in El Salvador, eighty-five percent of the abuses were attributed to the Reagan-assisted right-wing military and its death-squad allies.[176]

After a Contra re-supply plan was shot down in 1986, Abrams, along with the National Security Council's Oliver North and the CIA's Alan Fiers, appeared several times before Congressional hearings but withheld important information on the Administration's connection to the secret and private Contra-support network. Abrams ultimately copped a plea bargain with Independent Counsel Lawrence Walsh, pleading

....

176 Corn, David. "Elliott Abrams. It's Back!" *The Nation*, July 2, 2001. www.thenation.com/doc/20010702/corn

guilty to two misdemeanor counts of lying to Congress during the Iran Contra hearings. He was subsequently pardoned by George H.W. Bush.

Abrams is married to the daughter of Norman Podhoretz.

His current position did not require Senate approval.

Amal – This is a long-established Shiite political party whose name means "hope." Its historical objective has been to achieve greater respect for Lebanon's Shiites and to get a larger percentage of resources allocated to Shiite-dominated South Lebanon. Amal's 14,000 man militia fought a long campaign against Palestinian refugees in the Lebanese civil war called the War of the Camps.

Currently, Amal is aligned with Hezbollah against the Siniora government.

Michel Aoun – General Michel Aoun was named acting Prime Minister in 1988 in the last hours of Amine Gemayel's presidency because Lebanese leaders were unable to agree on a new president. In May 1989, Aoun declared war on Syria. This resulted in the deaths of 2,000 Lebanese. A thousand Lebanese and Syrian soldiers also died. Defeated, he chose exile in France. Aoun returned to Beirut in May 2005, formed the Free Patriotic Movement (FPM) and aligned himself with pro-Syrian Hezbollah to ensure his chances of not only winning in parliamentary elections but positioning himself as a future presidential candidate.

Baker-Hamilton Iraq Study Group Report – This report recommends that Syria cease all aid and arms shipments to Hezbollah, fully cooperate in investigations into political assassinations in Lebanon and cease efforts to undermine the democratically elected government of Lebanon. The study group also recommends that the Bush administration enter into talks with Syria and Iran. Given the right incentives, Syria has the ability to halt arms shipments to Hezbollah, thereby incapacitating any future military operations against Israel. President George W. Bush dismisses the idea of engaging Syria and Iran in dialogue, claiming that such overtures would reward the enemy.

According to former Secretary of State James Baker, "Negotiations are not a reward, nor are they a gift. They are rather a process in which two adversaries (or enemies) engage as a means to end the conflict between them."[177]

Bekaa Valley – The Bible describes Lebanon as the land of milk and honey because of its lush farmland. The Bekaa Valley, situated between Mount Lebanon and the Anti-Lebanon Mountains, was known as the breadbasket of the Roman Empire. The Bekaa is still Lebanon's most important farming region, generating some twelve percent of the country's GDP. It is home to Lebanon's renowned wines and is where the Romans first cultivated the Cabernet Sauvignon, a dark red grape, used to make the prized variety of red wine. The Bekaa's twelve wineries produce six million bottles of wine annually, exporting them to France and the US.

Baalbeck in the Bekaa Valley was founded as a crossroads of the caravan routes. The Roman temples of Bacchus and Jupiter, the remains of which still stand, were constructed using the biggest man-made stones in the world. In Lebanese folklore, people refer to Baalbeck as having been built by giants, for who else could have lifted such heavy weights? Aside from its magnificent Roman temples and its international summer music festival, Baalbeck is also home to a large Shiite population, many of whom are refugees from South Lebanon. It was here that the Iranian Revolutionary Guards trained the future Hezbollah fighters in the early 1980s.

Cairo Agreement – In 1969 the Lebanese government and the PLO signed the Cairo Agreement, which effectively endorsed the latter's freedom of movement in Lebanon to recruit, arm, train and employ fighters against Israel. The agreement gave the PLO the sole right to police its own camps and forbade the entry of any Lebanese authority, including the Lebanese Army, inside the camps. By signing such a document the Lebanese govern-

....

177 Eam, Josh and IPF Staff. "Engaging Syria Now." *IPF Focus*, Volume 4.46, December 21, 2006.

ment essentially washed its hands of South Lebanon. Worse, it became party to the Arab-Israeli conflict.

Demographics: Who lives where? – In South Lebanon, the region from Jezzine, forty kilometers north of the Israeli border, to Ras El Nakoura on the Israeli border, is sixty percent Shiite and thirty-five percent Christian. The Chouf, located southeast of Beirut, in that part of Mount Lebanon that rises dramatically from the Mediterranean to dominate the whole of Lebanon, is home to both Druze and Christians. Sunni Muslims and Christians, primarily Greek Orthodox, live along the coast from Tripoli in the north to Saida in the south.

Druze Religion – The Druze are a fiercely independent and secretive religious group mainly concentrated at the base of Mount Hermon, in the Chouf region between Beirut and Sidon, in northern Israel and the Golan Heights. Estimated to be about 750,000 members worldwide, the Druze religion was created out of Ismaili Islam. They are monotheistic and recognize seven prophets including Adam, Abraham and Jesus but reject the concept of a virgin birth. They believe that the soul is instantaneously reincarnated by being reborn into another human being. According to their beliefs, everyone has a choice to do good or evil and is free to choose right from wrong. Seven commandments guide them in their daily life: a truthful tongue, protection of their brethren, excision of fallacies, rejection of the villain and aggressor, adoration of the Lord at all times, cheerful acceptance of whatever comes from Him and spontaneous submission to His Will. The Druze are encouraged to marry within their own faith and to consider their spouse their equal. Their religious meetings are on Thursday, not Friday, and they do not follow the Five Pillars of Islam (recitation of the creed and prayers five times a day, donating to charity, fasting during the month of Ramadan and making the pilgrimage to Mecca). For these reasons, most Muslims do not consider them to be part of Islam.

False Flag Assassinations – This is an action in which the perpetrator intends for the blame to be placed on a different party. The term originally comes from the naval concept of flying another country's flag to deceive and confuse other ships. The most basic motive for a false flag incident would be to frame the enemy for an act of aggression in order to justify a supposed defensive response. Some observers of the Middle East suggest that the murders of Pierre Gemayel and the other anti-Syrian politicians were false flag assassinations and not the work of the Syrians as is currently alleged.

French Mandate – At the end of World War I, France and Britain carved up the Ottoman Empire. Britain was mandated Palestine; to France befell the area that is now Syria and Lebanon. In its mandate, France sought to increase its power over Syria by separating religious minorities, thereby weakening the nascent Arab nationalism already beginning to manifest itself in Damascus. France's original plan was to establish three sectarian states: one Alawi state in the north around the seaport of Lattakia; a Sunni Muslim state in the center and a Druze one to the south. The three were incorporated instead into present-day Syria.

France initially created Greater Lebanon, knitting together Mount Lebanon with the regions of Beirut, Tripoli, Sidon, Tyre and Akkar. However, wanting to maximize the area under its control, and encouraged by some Christian leaders, France pushed Lebanon's border to the "Anti-Lebanon" mountains on the far eastern side of the Bekaa Valley, an area that had been culturally linked to Damascus for hundreds of years. The demographics of Lebanon were profoundly altered by this maneuver because it added territory and contained people who were predominately Muslim or Druze. With these new additions Lebanese Christians constituted barely fifty percent of the population, while Sunnis saw their numbers increase eight-fold and the Shiites four-fold.

Gaza Strip – The Strip, approximately twenty-five miles long and seven miles wide, is home to 1.4 million Palestinians.

Samir Geagea – During the Lebanese civil war ('75–90) Geagea was one of Bachir Gemayel's top lieutenants. After Bachir's death in September 1982, Geagea took command of his Lebanese Forces militia. In 1989, when General Michel Aoun declared war on Syria, Geagea refused to join Aoun in what he considered a reckless adventure. Aoun subsequently declared war on Geagea and his men. Accused of perpetrating a church bombing and some political assassinations in the late '80s, Geagea was condemned to four life sentences. He spent eleven years in solitary confinement before being pardoned in July 2005. His followers believe the accusations made against him were fabricated by the Syrians whose military presence in Lebanon Geagea vehemently opposed. He currently sits in the anti-Syrian Siniora cabinet and has the support of fifty percent of Lebanese Christians; the other half are loyal to Michel Aoun.

Pierre Gemayel – He was thirty-six when he was assassinated on November 21, 2006. He descended from a long line of Lebanese politicians, including his grandfather and namesake who founded the Christian right-wing Phalange Party in 1939, which was modeled after the Nazi Youth Movement. His uncle, Bachir, was elected president in 1982 only to be assassinated a month later. His father, Amine, was elected president after Bachir's murder.

Golan Heights – The Golan is a region in southwestern Syria occupied by Israel since the June '67 war between Israel, Syria, Jordan and Egypt. Prior to the war the Golan was home to some 100,000 Syrians. In November 2006, Syria's President, Bachar al-Assad, offered to make peace with Israel in exchange for the return of the Golan Heights.

Hamas – This group was founded in 1987 out of the Muslim Brotherhood, a religious and political movement in Egypt in the 1970s. Its terrorist wing has carried out suicide bombings and attacks against Israelis. Hamas's first suicide bombing inside Israel took place in April 1993. Its annual budget of about $50 million comes from expatriates, Saudi Arabia and Iran. Ninety percent of this money supports Hamas's social services network which funds schools, orphanages, mosques, healthcare clinics, soup kitchens and sports leagues.

Today it is the Palestinians' largest and most influential movement. It was democratically elected into the Palestinian legislature in January 2006 running on an anti-corruption platform and pledging to improve people's lives. Hamas implicitly recognizes Israel on its pre-'67 borders.

Rafic Hariri – Hariri served as Lebanon's Prime Minister from 1992 to 2004. He was assassinated on February 14, 2005. A self-made billionaire, he was credited with the reconstruction of Beirut's center post-civil war. Under the guise of reconstruction, however, he formed a company called Solidere which assumed ownership of the city's center, thereby depriving thousands of small business owners of their property rights.

Hariri was also a philanthropist, distributing some 33,000 scholarships to students to study abroad. He built hospitals, mosques and schools throughout the country. A personal friend of French president Jacques Chirac, Hariri is said to have contributed some fifty million francs to Chirac's presidential campaign in 1995.

Hariri's assassination gave rise to Lebanon's "Cedar Revolution." Under pressure from the US and France, who along with Hariri co-authored UN Resolution 1559, Syria withdrew its troops from Lebanon ending a twenty-nine-year occupation.

Saad Hariri – He is Rafic Hariri's second son. He graduated from Georgetown University with an engineering degree. At the age of thirty-five, he runs Saudi Oger, a $3.3 billion construction conglomerate started by his father. His Future Bloc party won 72 (out of 128) parliamentary seats in the 2005 elections. Hezbollah accuses Hariri of collaborating with the Americans. Why else, they ask, would he have had two private audiences with President George W. Bush at the White House, the first in January 2006? On November 17, 2006, the Lebanese daily *Ad-Diyar* released a letter allegedly sent by the International Lebanese Committee to Saad Hariri on July 17, 2006, the fourth day of the Israeli-Hezbollah conflict. This letter would appear to back up Hezbollah's claims of collaboration between Hariri and the US. It says: "The agreed upon plan is to totally destroy Hezbollah's military structure and leave the mission of 'pressure' to the United States. After Hezbollah is destroyed, and not before, the US and France will present a draft resolution to the UN Security Council to deploy international forces on the Lebanese-Israeli and Lebanese-Syrian borders...The United States has decided that this campaign does not stop unless Hezbollah is totally crushed because destroying Hezbollah is a US priority especially if it is to go for a standoff with Iran."[178]

Hezbollah – Hezbollah, meaning Party of God, is a political and military party officially begun in 1985 as a local resistance movement against the Israeli occupation. Ronald Reagan's term for such movements in the late '80s was "freedom fighters," a local population struggling to free itself from the yolk of a military occupation. The United States and Israel, under George W. Bush and Ariel Sharon and his successor, Ehud Olmert, call Hezbollah a terrorist organization while the Arab and Muslim world considers it a legitimate militant Shiite political party.

Hezbollah claims that its initial idea of transforming Lebanon into an Islamic state has been abandoned in favor of a more inclusive approach. In a 1985 open letter to the Lebanese people Hezbollah stated: "We do not impose Islam on anyone as we hate those who impose their beliefs and regimes on us and we do not want Islam to reign in Lebanon by force."

Hezbollah receives financial support and weaponry from its mentor, Iran, the regional Shiite powerhouse. Hezbollah's relationship with Syria, on the other hand, is more nuanced. Syria supports Hezbollah's hard-line position against Israel. In return, Hezbollah underwrites Syria's domination of Lebanon.

....

178 Mussaoui, Fatima. "Lebanese Daily Publishes Letter to MP Saad Hariri during July War, with Plans to 'Terminate' Hezbollah." *Ad-Diyar*, December 9, 2007. http://palestinianpundit.blogspot.com/2006/11/lebanese-daily-publishes-letter-to-mp.html

Hezbollah has been linked to the American Embassy bomb-ing in Beirut in 1983 and to the Marine barracks bombing the same year. I have found no reliable source to confirm this alle-gation. Instead, what is confirmed is that both bombings were linked to Iranian-backed Islamic Jihadists (who were in the Bekaa Valley at the time training the nascent Hezbollah move-ment), some of whom may have later joined Hezbollah in 1985. CIA sources say that Islamic militants kidnapped Westerners in Beirut; they make no mention of Hezbollah.[179]

In June 2000, the Israeli Army withdrew from South Leb-anon, ending an 18-year occupation. Hezbollah's successful guerrilla campaign is credited with achieving the withdrawal. However, some of the credit also goes to a group of Israeli mothers called the Four Mothers Movement, who, furious at losing so many of their sons, forced then-Prime Minister Ehud Barak to withdraw his troops from South Lebanon.

Aside from its military wing, Hezbollah maintains a social service network which runs hospitals, free clinics and schools. After the Israeli-Hezbollah war ended in August 2006, the organization, with funds from Iran, distributed $12,000 to every family whose house was destroyed.

In November 2006, Hezbollah walked out of the Lebanese government. Their condition for returning was the formation of a new unity government with full veto power over any cab-inet decisions. While this is an attempt to increase its power, Hezbollah more than likely wants to make sure no govern-ment can ever force it to disarm. If it obtains veto power, this, of course, will never happen.

Hezbollah-Amal War – Hezbollah, a faith-based movement resented Amal's secular, non-clerical leadership and accom-modations with Lebanese politicos. Few were surprised when vicious battles exploded in the spring of '88 between the two

....

179 US Department of State. Background Information on Foreign Terrorist Organizations. www.state.gov/s/ct/rls/rpt/fto/2801.htm

militias with each side trying to win the hearts and minds of the Shiites in the South as well as in the teeming southern suburbs of Beirut where half the Shiite population lives.[180]

The fighting was sparked by the kidnapping of US Marine Lt. Colonel William Higgins, who was serving with UN forces in the south. The operation was carried out by a splinter group of Amal, a group which was actually sympathetic to Hezbollah. The Higgins incident threatened Amal's strategy of maintaining a cooperative working relationship with the UN troops in the south. Amal's attempts to find Higgins triggered serious clashes between Amal and Hezbollah, allowing Amal to momentarily consolidate its grip on southern Lebanon. As for the poor Higgins, he was brutally murdered by his captors.[181]

By the fall of '88, fighting erupted in the southern suburb of Beirut. Amal was badly defeated, losing virtually its entire military foothold in the capital.[182] By early '89 Hezbollah had also successfully curtailed Amal's influence in the south.[183]

The new Iranian leadership that emerged in the early 1990s was outraged by the internecine fighting between Amal and Hezbollah and pointedly condemned both sides for their actions.

Hezbollah-Aoun Bloc – In February 2006, Hezbollah leader Hassan Nasrallah and former General Michel Aoun of the Free Patriotic Movement signed a "memorandum of understanding" in which Hezbollah and Aoun agreed to cooperate on a great number of topics including reform of the electoral law, security, human rights and foreign relations. The collaboration between Hezbollah and Aoun is quite curious since Hezbollah is pro-Syrian and Michel Aoun, until he signed the "memorandum of understanding" with Hezbollah, was

....

180 Norton, Augustus Richard. *Hezbollah: A Short Story.* Princeton University Press, Princeton, 2007.

181 Ibid.

182 Ibid.

183 Ibid, p. 44.

staunchly anti-Syrian. Aoun's critics claim that he will do anything, even destabilize the country and turn Christians against
Christians, something that has already happened, to become
Lebanon's next president. Aoun defends his actions insisting
that Christians will never feel secure in Lebanon if they do not
deal pragmatically with the Muslim majority that now exists in
the country.

On November 11, 2006, the Hezbollah bloc walked out of
the government. They insisted on the formation of a new unity
government to include a total of eight from Hezbollah's block.
They also demand full veto power. This despite the fact that
of the more than 4,800 cabinet decisions taken by the Siniora
government before November 11, all but three were decided by
consensus. Currently Hezbollah holds two ministerial positions. An additional four cabinet members, three Shiite and
one Christian from Aoun's bloc, forms the six member pro-
Hezbollah bloc.

Inter-Christian Conflict – In November, when the Hezbollah-
Aoun coalition walked out of the government, approximately
fifty percent of Christians supported Michel Aoun and praised
his decision to support Hezbollah over the Siniora government, which they consider corrupt and an instrument of the
US government. Though exact figures are hard to come by,
Aoun's supporters are less enamored with the General after six
months of government stalemate with no solution in sight.

The other half of Lebanon's Christian community bitterly
opposed Aoun's alliance with Hezbollah, an Islamic organization they regard as a threat to Lebanon's Christians.

Iran – Since the early '80s Iran has played a pivotal role in Lebanese politics. It helped train Hezbollah. It continues to supply
the movement with its weapons and it even directs its military and political operations. Middle East observers believe
that in July 2006, during the Israeli-Hezbollah war, that Iran
used Hezbollah in a proxy war with America, the latter using
Israel as its proxy. Since the war ended with no clear winner,

these same observers fear another round of bloody conflict. On the political scene, Iran is pushing Hezbollah to acquire more political power in Lebanon, thus spreading Shiite influence and Iranian ideology. Because the Iranian President purportedly advocates the destruction of the State of Israel, the Jewish State, in turn, advocates a strong stance against Iran. The fear, however, is that such a position could translate into a regional war that would be fought in Lebanon again. A far better option would be the adoption of the Baker-Hamilton Iraq Study Group's proposal, which suggests direct talks with Iran.

Iranian Revolutionary Guards – This is the largest branch of the Islamic Republic of Iran's military. It is, in fact, separate from the regular Army, Navy and Air Force and is equipped with its own ground forces. It controls the Basij militia, which has a potential strength of eleven million, although it essentially consists of only 90,000 regular soldiers and 300,000 reservists. The force's main role is in national security, including internal and border security, as well as law enforcement. It is also responsible for Iran's missile defense systems. The Iranian Revolutionary Guard was formed as a force loyal to Ayatollah Khomeini when he came to power in 1979 and only became a full military force alongside the regular army in the Iran-Iraq War (1980–88). It is infamous for its human wave attacks in Basra during the Iran-Iraq War.

Iran's current president, Mahmoud Ahmadinejad, was a member of the Revolutionary Guard.

Emile Lahoud – Pro-Syrian Emile Lahoud was due to step down as Lebanon's president in 2004, at the end of his six-year term. Instead, Syria insisted his presidency be extended another three years. Intense pressure was brought to bear on the Lebanese parliament who finally acquiesced to Syria's demand. Then-Prime Minister Rafic Hariri resigned his post to protest Syria's heavy handedness.

Lebanese Constitution – This document seemingly specifies the balance of power between the various religious groups. France, however, designed the constitution to guarantee the political dominance of its Christian allies. The President had to be a Maronite Christian, the Prime Minister a Sunni Muslim and the Speaker of the Parliament a Shiite. On the basis of the 1932 census, which was designed to favor the Christians over the Muslims, the seats in parliament were divided according to a 6:5 Christian-Muslim ratio. The constitution also gave the president veto power over any legislation approved by parliament, virtually ensuring that the 6:5 ratio would not be revised in the event that the population distribution changed. The population balance did indeed change; by the mid-60s, the Muslims were the majority. The Christians' refusal to address the issue of veto power infuriated the Muslims and was one of the factors which contributed to Lebanon's civil war.

Lebanon – The name is derived from the Semitic root LBN, which is linked to the word white, a reference, no doubt, to the snow-covered Mount Lebanon.

Lebanon's 2005 Elections (the first in 30 years) – The most important consequence of the 2005 elections is that it brought the **anti-Syrian** Hariri Bloc, led by Rafic Hariri's son, Saad, into power with a majority seventy-two of the 128 available seats. Included in the anti-Syrian Hariri Bloc are: Druze leader Walid Jumblatt of the Progressive Socialist Party with fifteen seats and Samir Geagea, leader of the Christian Lebanese Forces with six seats.

The **pro-Syrian** bloc that includes principally Hezbollah and Amal, the two Shiite parties, won thirty-five seats. General Michel Aoun's Free Patriotic Movement, which won twenty seats, is also part of the pro-Syrian bloc. Despite his party's impressive gains, Aoun was not invited to join Siniora's government.

Lebanon now has an anti-Syrian Sunni Muslim Prime Minister, Fouad Siniora, and a pro-Syrian Christian president, Emile Lahoud.

The Levant – Lebanon and Syria are called the Levant states. The term *Levant* derives from the Middle French *levant*, the participle of *lever*, "to rise," as in *soleil levant*, "sun rising." Levant equates to the Arabic term *Mashriq*, "the land of the rising sun."

March 8 Coalition – The pro-Syrian Hezbollah-Aoun bloc.

March 14th, 2005 – The largest street demonstration in Lebanon's history, a month after the assassination of former Prime Minister Rafic Hariri. The protest was over Syria's twenty-nine-year occupation and Syria's suspected role in Hariri's murder. This demonstration was also called the **Cedar Revolution.**

March 14th Coalition – Those who pushed for the withdrawal of Syrian troops from Lebanon, i.e. Prime Minister Fouad Siniora, Saad Hariri, Walid Jumblatt and Samir Geagea.

Maronites – Maronites, one of the principal Christian religious groups in Lebanon, are members of Eastern Catholic Church. Their heritage dates back to Maroun, a 4th Century monk, who died in 423. Before the Muslim conquest (634–640), Maronites spoke a dialect of Aramaic, the language of Christ, and have only been an Arabic-speaking community since approximately the 9th Century. Syriac-Aramaic, however, still remains the liturgical language of the Maronite Church. Approximately 850,000 Maronites out of a total two million world-wide currently live in Lebanon. This represents about twenty-seven percent of the total number of Christians in Lebanon. In 1648, when the Druze began persecuting the Christians in their mountain villages, France declared itself protector of the Christians of Lebanon. France's close ties with the Maronites was one of the central foundations for the creation of the state of Lebanon.

Mount Lebanon and Anti-Lebanon – The Mount Lebanon range rises dramatically from the narrow coast along the Mediterranean to dominate the whole of Lebanon before dropping eastward into the fertile Bekaa Valley. The Anti-Lebanon, which begins at the eastern edge of the Bekaa, is an arid mountain range that forms part of Lebanon's eastern border with Syria.

Hassan Nasrallah – He is the spiritual and political leader of Hezbollah. In 1982, Nasrallah was expelled from Amal, another Shiite movement, headed even back then by Nabih Berri, the current Speaker of the Lebanese Parliament, for criticizing the weaknesses and indecisions of Amal's leaders during the '82 Israeli invasion. Nasrallah joined the newly formed Hezbollah in 1985 but left shortly thereafter to study Shiite Islam in Qom, Iran. He was only twenty-nine when he returned to Lebanon in 1989 and joined Hezbollah's central command. In 1997, his oldest son, Hadi, nineteen, died fighting the Israeli Army in South Lebanon.

In a nationally televised speech on July 22, 2006, Nasrallah claimed that had he known that Israel would respond with such force he would not have ordered the kidnapping of the Israeli soldiers on July 12. On the other hand, Nasrallah must have known from past border skirmishes to expect some kind of Israeli reprisal. It is therefore hard to comprehend why Nasrallah chose this particular moment to act. Was it a terrible miscalculation as he stated or was he acting on orders from Iran?

Neo-conservative – Neo-conservatives, including many Jewish and Catholic intellectuals, are part of a US-based political movement rooted in liberal Cold War anticommunism and a backlash to the social liberation movements of the '60s and '70s. They have since drifted toward conservatism, thus they are new (neo) conservatives. They favor an aggressive unilateral US foreign policy. Many members of the Bush administration are neo-cons closely associated with Norman Podhoretz, the dean of neo-conservatism, William Kristol's *The Weekly Standard*, *Commentary*, the American Enterprise Institute (AEI), the Project for the New American Century (PNAC) and the Jewish Institute for National Security (JNSA).

Northern Israel – The mountainous Galilee Region dominates Northern Israel, extending twenty-five miles from the Mediterranean to the Sea of Galilee (also called Lake Tiberias). The major cities include Tiberias, Haifa, Acre, Nazareth and Ein Hod. There are approximately 7,150,000 people living in Israel. Of that total, seventy-five percent are Jews and twenty percent are Palestinian or Arab Israelis (designated as such by the Israeli government.) Of the 2,030,469 people living in northern Israel, 651,521 are Palestinian.

Occupation Zones – The Israeli occupation of South Lebanon extended from Naqoura on the Mediterranean coast just inside Lebanon up to Mount Hermon and the Litani River, an area that covered from south to northeast some hundred kilometers by eight to twenty kilometers. This enclave of some 100,000 people, sixty percent Shiite and thirty-five percent Christian, was placed under the command of Major Saad Haddad after the breakup of the Lebanese Army in 1976. Israel ended its occupation in May 2000.

The Syrian occupation of Lebanon extended, at various times, from Beirut to Tripoli in the north, and from Beirut south to Sidon and into the Bekaa Valley. All in all, the Syrian occupation at one time or another encompassed almost 90 percent of Lebanese territory. Syria finally withdrew its last troops in April 2005 ending a twenty-nine-year occupation.

PLO – At a summit in Cairo, Arab leaders in 1964 called for the creation of the Palestinian Liberation Organization. The charter did not stipulate that the Palestinian people had the right to self-determination or, if necessary, the right to fight to regain the UN-promised portion of the original Palestine. The Arab leaders' intention in creating the PLO was to control the resistance movements so as not to be drawn into a conflict with the State of Israel. Yasser Arafat formed a militia called Fatah in 1965. He believed that the Palestinians could count only on themselves and that the only realistic way of regaining the portion of Palestine they had lost was through armed struggle. Arafat became President of the Executive Committee of the PLO in 1969.

In 1970 King Hussein expelled Arafat and his PLO from Jordan because the PLO repeatedly attacked Israel from bases there. The king reasoned that if he did not restrain the PLO that Israel would destroy his country. Arafat moved his PLO headquarters to the Saba-Chatilla refugee camps in Beirut.

Pre-1967 border, also called the Green Line or the 1949 Armistice Line – After the cessation of hostilities between the Arab countries and Israel in 1948, an armistice agreement was signed in 1949. The agreement delineated the borders of each party and designated the no man's land between them according to the location of the respective armies. This line demarcated the border between Israel and the West Bank and the Gaza Strip as recognized by the international community even though Israel did not specify, nor has it ever specified, the specific boundaries of its state. Although the line became known later as the Green Line or, more commonly, the pre-'67 border, its proper name is the 1949 Armistice Line.

During the June 1967 Arab-Israeli War, Israel crossed the Green Line to occupy the West Bank, the Gaza Strip and the Sinai, East Jerusalem and the Golan Heights. UN Resolution 242, adopted in November 1967, called for the withdrawal of Israeli forces from territories occupied during the 1967 war in return for an Arab pledge of full peace and recognition.

Jordan and Egypt, in exchange for the return of the Sinai, have signed peace treaties with Israel. Arafat recognized Israel's right to exist in 1978 and offered full peace. In June 2007, Hamas recognized Israel's right to exist "on its pre-'67 borders." The Saudi Initiative, signed by twenty-two Muslim nations and agreed to in March 2002, recognized Israel's right to exist and offered it full diplomatic and economic relations if it agreed to withdraw to its pre-'67 border. The initiative even agreed to minor border justifications that could include some of the Israeli settlements illegally built in Arab East Jerusalem. The Geneva Initiative, proposed by a group of distinguished Israelis and Palestinians, suggested similar conditions in October 2003 in return for Israel's withdrawal of the Occupied West Bank. Israel has yet to respond to either of these overtures.

Religious Majorities – Lebanon has a population of approximately 3.4 million people. Sixty percent are Muslim and of that figure forty percent are Shiite. The rest of the remaining sixty percent are Sunni. The Druze represent less than five percent of the population. Christians make up thirty-five percent of the population, the Maronites being the largest component. The population balance of power has shifted in Lebanon over recent decades. Large numbers of Lebanese, mostly Christians, emigrated during Lebanon's civil war while within the Shiite community birth rates rose.

Fouad Siniora – He was Rafic Hariri's right hand man in business and politics for forty-five years. Like Hariri, he grew up in Sidon in a Sunni Muslim family. During the 1970s he lectured at American University of Beirut and the Lebanese University. The Hezbollah bloc blames Siniora, because of his close ties with Rafic Hariri, for the country's $43 billion debt. Given that electricity shortages are incessant, that the water delivery system is antiquated and non-potable and private education is out of reach for the average Lebanese, Hezbollah and its disenfranchised Shiite majority are right to criticize past and present policies that appear to cater only to the rich. Siniora is also accused of taking orders from the American Ambassador in Beirut, of failing to send the Lebanese Army to the south during the war with Israel, and of inviting Secretary of State Rice to Beirut without insisting first that she call for an immediate cease-fire.

South Lebanese Army – The SLA, headed by former Christian Lebanese Army Major Saad Haddad and his militia of some 2,000 men, acted as Israel's proxy army in South Lebanon from 1978 to 2000. The SLA brutally repressed the local civilian population of some 100,000, sixty percent of whom are Shiites, the rest Christians. The worst outrage took place in Khiam, a village near the Israeli border, where Haddad's men herded Shiite Muslim men, women and children into a mosque, killing all seventy of them in cold blood. Under the supervision of Israeli officers, the SLA also operated a notorious prison in Khiam where torture and solitary confinement were the norm.

South Lebanon and Its People – This is a region extending from the Awali River in the uppermost part of South Lebanon to Ras el Nakoura in the south, a distance of some fifty kilometers, and from the Mediterranean Sea in the west to the Syrian-Lebanese border in the northeast, some one hundred kilometers away. Some of the south's best-known towns include: Jezzine, Sidon, Tyre, Nabatieh, Marjayoun, Hasbaya, Bint Jbeil and Nakoura on the Israeli border. Sixty percent of South Lebanon's residents are Shiites; the rest are Christians. During the Israeli-Hezbollah war, some 800,000 residents from South Lebanon were forced to flee their homes.

Sunni-Shiite Split – In 632 A.D. the Prophet Muhammad died at the age of sixty-three. Twenty-nine years after his death, in 661 A.D., a rivalry began between Sunnis and those who would call themselves Shiites. The dispute was over who should have rightfully succeeded Muhammad. At the time of Muhammad's death, all Muslims followed the tribal tradition where a council of elders chose the most senior or respected elder to become head of the Islamic community.[184] Abu Bakr, who was Muhammad's father-in-law and close confidant, was chosen as successor. Though a small group believed that Muhammad's cousin and son-in-law, Ali ibn Abi Talib, was more qualified for the job, they ultimately accepted Abu Bakr's leadership.[185] Caliph Abu Bakr was ultimately succeeded by Caliphs Umar Uthman and finally Ali. The reign of these four men spanned the years 632 A.D. to 661 A.D. The split started in 661 A.D. when Ali was assassinated. The Shiite sect of Islam was born at the siege and battle of Karbala in 680, when Ali's son Husayn and seventy-two of his companions and family members were massacred by the soldiers of the second Umayyad caliph, Yazid I. The word Shiite means "followers of Ali."[186]

In fact, three events – Ali's murder, the transformation of the caliphate into a monarchy, and the de facto separation of

....

184 Nasr, Vali. *The Shia Revival.* W.W. Norton & Co., New York, 2007, p. 35.
185 Ibid.
186 Ibid, p. 40.

religious and political authorities under the Umayyads – led a minority of Muslims, who opposed these changes, to also reject the legitimacy of the first three Caliphs. This minority who would became the first Shiites argued that Muhammad's family members were the true leaders of the Muslim community, for the blood of the Prophet ran in their veins and they alone bore his charisma and the spiritual qualities vested in him by God.[187] According to them, Muhammad chose Ali as his successor because Muhammad said, "Whoever recognized me as his master will recognize Ali as his master."[188] Ali had two sons, Hassan and Husayn. While both died violently, it was Husayn's beheading by the Caliph's army in the battle if Karbala (in present-day Iraq) in 680 A.D. that is commemorated today by Shiites in the great feast of mourning, remembrance and atonement called Ashoura.[189]

We see these ancient animosities playing themselves out in the streets of Iraq. Shiites, who head Iraq's government, are closely aligned with Shiite-dominated Iran and with Hezbollah in Lebanon. In the predominately Sunni nations like Saudi Arabia, Jordan and Egypt, also known in the region as American puppet regimes, there is great trepidation over a Shiite revival throughout the Middle East. While there are 1.3 billion Muslims worldwide, the majority of whom are Sunni, in the area from Lebanon to the Persian Gulf the ratio is closer to 50:50. In Bahrain's recent elections, Shiites made major gains. In the event that America decides to pull out of Iraq, Saudi Arabia has already promised their Sunni brethren in Iraq military support; Iran has done the same, reassuring the Shiites they will have military support anytime they need it.

Taif Agreement – As a result of almost fifteen years of civil war, Lebanese leaders agreed on a charter of national reconcilia-

....

187 Ibid, p. 37.
188 Ibid.
189 Ibid, p.44.

tion in 1989 known as the Taif Agreement. It declared that the Prime Minister, who is always a Sunni, would now be responsible to the Parliament and not to the President, who is always a Maronite, thereby weakening the Presidency and the power of the Christians. Taif also agreed that the Parliament, also known as the Chamber of Deputies, would be increased from 99 to 128 members with the seats equally divided between Christian and Muslims. The Taif agreement also advocated the abolition of political sectarianism but provided no timeframe or mechanism for its implementation. It also called for Syrian troops to reposition themselves in the Bekaa Valley, for Christian militias to surrender their weapons and Hezbollah, operating in South Lebanon, to keep their arms until Israel abided by UN Resolution 425, which calls for the immediate withdrawal of Israeli troops from Lebanese territory.

UN Resolution 1559 – This resolution calls on Lebanon to establish its sovereignty over all its land, for all foreign forces to withdraw from Lebanon and for all militias to disband. Lebanon has demanded that Israel withdraw from the Shebaa Farms area, that they release all Lebanese detainees in Israeli prisons and that they hand over maps detailing the whereabouts of some 140,000 mines left by Israel during its '82–2000 occupation as preconditions for fully implementing UN Resolution 1559.

INDEX